UNSHACKLED VOICES

OF FORGOTTEN FATHERS THAT SPEAK TO HOUSE OFFICIALS AND COMMUNITY

By

YARAH & SAMUEL BEN ISRAEL

Preface

Introduction

In the land of lost dreams and broken promises, there exists a group of men who have been cast aside and forgotten by society. These are not the same men who once walked through those iron gates, their spirits broken and their souls shattered. No, these men have transformed themselves within the confines of their incarceration, becoming warriors of change and symbols of hope for the future.

For over 25 years that I know of, these incarcerated fathers have toiled behind bars, completing more programs than the state of Florida can remember offering. They have amassed over 15 program compilations, dedicated over 10 years to mentoring others, and yet, they remain imprisoned within the failing fatherless households across the state. The question that lingers in the stale air of the prison cells is this: does the state of Florida truly believe in its system and programs, or are they merely designed to keep these men confined within the walls for the rest of their days?

Are our voters being fed half-truths and sugar-coated lies, shielding them from the harsh reality of a system that may be more focused on profit than rehabilitation? The shackle voices of the incarcerated fathers are rising, ready to tell their stories and plead for a chance at redemption and renewal. Join me on this journey as we uncover the hidden truths and untold tales of those who have been silenced for far too long.

Table of Contents

Chapter 1:
Awakening Florida's Consciousness

T he sun rises over the vast expanse of Florida, casting a golden glow upon its diverse landscape. As the state awakens to a new day, a collective stirring can be felt in the air, a sense of awakening that is palpable to all who call this place home.

The time has come to confront the shadows of the past, to acknowledge the harsh realities that have long been buried beneath the surface. It is a time for reflection, for introspection, and for a reckoning with the truths that have been swept aside in favor of a more comfortable narrative.

Florida's consciousness is stirring, like a dormant beast roused from slumber. The whispers of history echo through the streets, reminding its inhabitants of the untold stories, the forgotten voices, and the wounds that still fester beneath the surface.

It is a moment of clarity, a realization that the past can no longer be ignored, that the pain of generations past must be acknowledged and addressed. The awakening is not without its challenges, for it requires courage, humility, and a willingness to face the uncomfortable truths that lie in wait.

But as the sun climbs higher in the sky, casting its light upon the land, there is a glimmer of hope, a sense of renewal that permeates the air. This is a time of reckoning, yes, but also a time of opportunity – an opportunity to heal, to grow, and to forge a new path forward.

As Florida's consciousness continues to stir, there is a sense of anticipation in the air, a feeling that change is on the horizon. The journey ahead will not be easy, but it is necessary – for only by confronting the past can the state truly move forward into a brighter, more inclusive future.

In the heart of Florida, within the confines of its prison walls, a chorus of voices rises, seeking to be heard and understood. These voices belong to the incarcerated men whose stories have long been silenced, their struggles ignored, and their humanity overshadowed by their mistakes.

It is time to embrace these voices, to listen with compassion and respect, and to acknowledge the profound impact of incarceration on individuals, families, and communities. Their stories are not just a collection of crimes and sentences, but a complex tapestry of circumstances, choices, and experiences that have led them to where they are today.

To truly awaken Florida's consciousness, it is essential to confront the reality of mass incarceration and its disproportionate impact on marginalized communities. This is not a time for finger-pointing or blame, but a time for problem-solving and healing. It is a time to recognize the humanity of those behind bars, to empathize with their struggles, and to work towards creating a more just and equitable system for all.

By amplifying the voices of the incarcerated men, we can begin to bridge the divide between those inside and outside the prison walls. Their experiences, insights, and perspectives are invaluable in shaping policies, programs, and initiatives that aim to break the cycle of incarceration and support rehabilitation and reintegration.

As Florida embraces the voices of the incarcerated, a new narrative begins to take shape – one of empathy, understanding, and collective responsibility. It is a narrative that acknowledges the inherent dignity of every individual, regardless of their past mistakes, and that seeks to create a society where all are given the opportunity to heal, grow, and thrive.

Together, we can build a future where justice is truly restorative, where compassion is the guiding principle, and where the voices of the marginalized are not just heard, but valued and respected. This is the path towards true transformation, towards a Florida that embodies the ideals of justice, empathy, and equality for all.

In the state of Florida, honesty is a powerful tool that can lead to healing, understanding, and ultimately, reunion with loved ones. For the incarcerated men yearning to reconnect with their children, the path to reconciliation begins with a commitment to truth-telling and transparency.

It is a common lament among those behind bars that they have been kept in the dark, fed misinformation, and denied the chance to fully understand their situations. As they grapple with the consequences of their actions and the impact on their families, the truth becomes a beacon of hope – a guiding light that can illuminate the path towards redemption and reunion.

But truth is a delicate and elusive thing, especially within the confines of an incarceration system marked by secrecy, stigma, and misinformation. The truths that are not being told to the incarcerated men – and by extension, to their families – often revolve around the complexities of their cases, the challenges they face in navigating the legal system, and the barriers to reentry and rehabilitation upon release.

To return to their children with honesty and integrity, the incarcerated men must first confront these hidden truths, both within themselves and within the system that governs their lives. They must acknowledge the mistakes they have made, take accountability for their actions, and seek avenues for personal growth and transformation.

At the same time, Florida must also grapple with its own truths – the harsh realities of mass incarceration, the disparities in sentencing and treatment, and the need for systemic reform to promote rehabilitation and reintegration. Only by confronting these uncomfortable truths can the state truly serve the best interests of its citizens, including those behind bars and their families.

As Florida embarks on a journey of honesty, truth, and reconciliation, the incarcerated men and their families are presented with a rare opportunity for healing and reunion. By embracing the power of truth-telling, they can forge new connections, rebuild trust, and pave the way for a brighter future filled with hope, understanding, and love.

Together, let us seek the truths that have long been hidden, let us confront the injustices that have long been ignored, and let us work towards a Florida that values honesty, integrity, and compassion in all aspects of its incarceration system. This is the path towards true healing, understanding, and reunion with our loved ones – a path that we must walk together, hand in hand, towards a future of hope and possibility.

Poem

I share with you a poem titled "Ol' Lady Justice, I had a dream," a reflection on the long sentencing practices in Florida courtrooms and the impact they have on lives hanging in the balance of one moment's decision.

I had a dream, a vision of a world where justice is not blind but sees the stark reality of fatherless homes and rising crime rates across America, particularly in the state of Florida. It matters not which governor or mayor we elect, for the root of the problem runs deeper than political office can reach. It is a problem that only a father, a figure of wisdom and compassion, can truly understand and rectify.

We are all humans, fallible and prone to making mistakes. Let us not forget the times when we have erred, when we have made choices that led us astray. Let us approach the issue of long sentencing with empathy and understanding, recognizing that those serving these sentences are not beyond redemption or deserving of a lifetime of suffering.

Mr. Rule Maker, I implore you to consider the hand that fate has dealt to those languishing behind bars, to envision a system that allows for second chances and paths to redemption. Let us not turn a blind eye to the potential for change and growth within every individual, no matter the mistakes of their past.

We exist in large numbers, united by our shared humanity and the capacity for transformation. It is time to make decisions that reflect the values of compassion and justice, to provide a way back for those who have made strides towards bettering themselves and society.

Let us come together, let us stand united in our pursuit of a fairer and more humane justice system. Let us heed the call of Ol' Lady Justice, to remove her blindfold not in ignorance, but in a quest for truth and righteousness. Together, let us pave the way for a brighter future, where long sentences in Florida courtrooms become a thing of the past.

I urge each of you to embrace the spirit of change, to advocate for a system that uplifts rather than condemns, and to stand in solidarity with those who seek redemption and a chance to make amends.

Chapter 2:
Florida's Time for Awakening:
Embracing Shared Responsibilities for a Brighter Future

In the heart of Florida, a new dawn is approaching – a moment of awakening that beckon both the lawmakers and the incarcerated fathers to embrace their shared responsibilities in shaping a brighter future for the children and families affected by incarceration. As the sun rises over the state, casting its golden light on the challenges and opportunities that lie ahead, a call to action resounds in the air: it is time for Florida to come together in unity and purpose, to mend the fractures that have divided communities and families, and to build a path towards healing and reconciliation.

For too long, the burden of responsibility has been unevenly distributed, with the weight of incarceration falling heavily on the shoulders of the incarcerated fathers and their families. As these men grapple with the consequences of their actions and the separation from their loved ones, the true impact of their incarceration reverberates through their homes and communities, casting shadows of pain, loss, and uncertainty.

But now, in this moment of awakening, a new narrative begins to unfold – one that recognizes the collective responsibility shared by all members of society, from the legislators crafting laws to the incarcerated fathers seeking redemption. It is a narrative of partnership and collaboration, in which each stakeholder plays a vital role in fostering a supportive environment for families, promoting rehabilitation and reentry, and ensuring the well-being of the children affected by incarceration.

As the lawmakers in Florida consider the policies and practices that shape the state's incarceration system, they are called upon to approach their work with compassion, empathy, and a commitment to justice. By enacting laws that prioritize rehabilitation over punishment, that address the root causes of crime, and that support the reintegration of formerly incarcerated individuals into society, they can positively impact the lives of countless families and children, offering them a pathway to a brighter future filled with hope and opportunity.

Simultaneously, the incarcerated fathers themselves are challenged to take responsibility for their actions, to seek redemption and personal growth, and to uphold their roles as fathers and mentors to their children. By engaging in rehabilitative programs, cultivating positive relationships with their families, and demonstrating a commitment to change, these men can pave the way for a successful reentry into society and a reconnection with their loved ones.

As Florida awakens to the shared responsibilities that bind its communities together, a new chapter unfolds – one characterized by collaboration, compassion, and the collective pursuit of a brighter future for all. It is a chapter in which the lawmakers and the incarcerated fathers stand side by side, hand in hand, working together towards a common goal of healing, reconciliation, and empowerment. This is the time for Florida to embrace its potential for change, to forge a path towards a more just and inclusive society, and to build a legacy of hope and possibility for generations to come.

As incarcerated individuals, we carry a dual responsibility – not only to address the present challenges we face, but also to lay the groundwork for a successful future beyond the confines of prison walls. While the journey towards rehabilitation and eventual release may seem daunting and uncertain, it is imperative that we remain steadfast in our commitment to personal growth, education, and self-improvement. What we do now behind bars is only the beginning of what needs to be done upon release, and it is essential that we continue to cultivate the skills and mindset necessary for a smooth transition back into society.

In the midst of incarceration, where time can feel stagnant and opportunities limited, it is easy to succumb to despair and hopelessness. However, it is precisely in these challenging circumstances that the seeds of our future success can be sown. By embracing a mindset of continuous learning and personal development, we can transform our time behind bars into a period of self-discovery, reflection, and growth.

Education, in all its forms, becomes our greatest ally in this journey of self-betterment. Whether through formal academic programs, vocational training, or self-directed study, we have the power to expand our knowledge, skills, and perspectives – laying a solid foundation for the challenges and opportunities that await us upon release. By equipping ourselves with the tools necessary to navigate the complexities of the outside world, we empower ourselves to seize new opportunities, pursue meaningful careers, and contribute positively to our communities.

Moreover, as we strive to create for ourselves a brighter future, it is essential that we remain proactive and intentional in our efforts. We must seize every opportunity for growth and development, whether through participating in rehabilitative programs, engaging in mentorship and counseling, or building positive relationships with our fellow incarcerated individuals. By surrounding ourselves with a supportive community of peers and mentors, we can draw strength, guidance, and inspiration to propel us forward on our journey of transformation and renewal.

Ultimately, our goal is not only to secure our own redemption and reintegration into society but also to keep the door of opportunity open for others who follow in our footsteps. By demonstrating a commitment to personal growth, resilience, and positive change, we set a powerful example for those around us — inspiring hope, courage, and determination in the face of adversity.

As we continue to learn, grow, and create for ourselves behind bars, we pave the way for a future filled with promise, potential, and possibility. Let us embrace this opportunity for transformation, let us seize the power of knowledge and self-improvement, and let us keep the doors of opportunity unlocked, ready to step into a brighter tomorrow upon our release.

Chapter 3:
Cutting down the rooted issues

The relationship between fathers and their children is a fundamental bond that has the power to shape the lives of both parties in profound ways. However, for many incarcerated fathers, this connection is often strained or severed due to the challenges of incarceration. In order to address this issue and promote healing and reunification, a holistic approach that combines character-based mentorship inside and outside of prisons is crucial.

Rooted issues such as family separation, lack of trust, and communication breakdowns must be addressed as a foundational step in the process of reconnecting fathers with their children. By implementing fatherhood initiatives that focus on character-building and mentorship classes within prisons and in society, we can create a supportive environment that nurtures personal growth, fosters positive values, and promotes healthy relationships.

Through more funding and resources allocated towards fatherhood initiatives, we can empower incarcerated fathers to develop the skills and mindset necessary to rebuild trust and establish a positive connection with their children. By providing access to mentorship programs that focus on character development, emotional intelligence, and effective communication, we can equip fathers with the tools they need to navigate the challenges of reintegration and family reunification.

Moreover, by involving families in the rehabilitation process and emphasizing the importance of understanding and empathy towards those impacted by incarceration, we can begin to heal the wounds of separation and miscommunication that have strained relationships. By encouraging open dialogue, fostering mutual respect, and promoting accountability, we can create a pathway towards forgiveness, healing, and reconciliation for both families and communities.

Ultimately, by instilling a sense of purpose, responsibility, and accountability in incarcerated fathers through character-based mentorship, we can empower them to make positive changes in their lives and relationships. By fostering a culture of respect, empathy, and understanding, we can break down barriers, rebuild trust, and promote healing within families and communities affected by incarceration.

It is through the recognition of each individual's inherent value, dignity, and potential for growth that we can create a more just and compassionate society. By embracing the power of mentorship, character development, and family reunification, we can pave the way for a brighter future for all individuals impacted by incarceration. Let us move forward with empathy, understanding, and a commitment to healing and reconciliation, guided by the belief that every individual has the capacity for redemption and renewal.

Within the Department of Corrections, a profound imperative emerges: the urgent need to provide a beacon of light for the incarcerated men seeking a way out of their past mistakes and towards a brighter future. Recently, a powerful moment unfolded when an individual serving a life sentence shared his story with the Jack Brewer team, revealing how witnessing his fellow inmates successfully reintegrate into society after completing their sentences sparked a glimmer of hope within his own heart. This poignant experience underscored the profound truth that the mere façade of progress—emulating change without embodying it—yields hollow, unsustainable results.

The essence of true metamorphosis lies in a complex tapestry woven from threads of change, determination, love, and compassion, interwoven with profound gratitude and reverence for a higher power like Yahweh. This transformative process is not a solitary journey; rather, it is a communal effort that calls upon legislators in the state of Florida to actively engage in fostering and perpetuating this emergent sense of hope that formerly incarcerated individuals are extending. In joining the movement towards redemption and rehabilitation, we collectively affirm our commitment to nurturing the belief within prisoners that their inherent capacity for growth and change is not only possible but worthy of pursuit.

The call to action resounds louder and clearer than ever within the Department of Corrections: it is time to shift from a punitive paradigm towards a holistic approach centered on redemption and rehabilitation. By cultivating an environment that cherishes second chances and accompanies individuals on their transformative paths, we can establish a system that not only reshapes lives but also empowers individuals to serve as catalysts for positive change within their communities. Let us heed this clarion call and stand united in our resolve to construct a future imbued with hope, healing, and transformation for all individuals ensnared by the complexities of the criminal justice system.

Chapter 4:
Healing Fathers and Families

T he journey towards healing the relationships between fathers and their families is a complex and challenging one. This process requires a deliberate and thoughtful approach to reestablishing fathers as the leaders of their households, a role that many are eager to embrace. However, this transition cannot be taken lightly and will require careful supervision and support to ensure its success.

One crucial aspect of this healing process is the need for increased communication and connection between fathers and their children. Letter writing can be a powerful tool in facilitating this connection, allowing fathers to express their thoughts and feelings to their children in a meaningful way. In addition, providing more opportunities for fathers to visit with their kids can help strengthen the bond between them and initiate the healing process.

Furthermore, counseling will play a key role in supporting both children and fathers as they navigate this transition. By providing a safe space for them to process their emotions, address any underlying issues, and learn effective communication strategies, counseling can help prevent potential conflicts and misunderstandings that may arise during this challenging time.

It is essential that this transition is overseen and managed effectively to avoid any potential pitfalls or setbacks. Without proper supervision and support, the healing process could become a source of stress and conflict for both fathers and children, leading to failure in reestablishing their relationships.

In conclusion, healing the relationships between fathers and their families is a delicate process that requires patience, compassion, and support. By implementing strategies such as letter writing, increased visitation, and counseling, we can help fathers and children navigate this transition successfully and build stronger, healthier relationship for the future

Dear Ones in Control,

We, the fatherless children of the world, come to you today with a message that carries the weight of our broken hearts, but also the glimmer of hope that burns within us. We acknowledge the mistakes of our fathers, the wrongs they have committed that have led to their absence from our lives. Yet, we implore you to see beyond their past transgressions and to recognize the potential for redemption and transformation that lies within them.

1. Our fathers have confessed their wrongdoings, and they now understand the profound impact their actions have had on our lives. They have expressed sincere remorse and a deep desire to make amends.

2. We have witnessed the change in their demeanor, the newfound determination to become the role models we so desperately need. They yearn to guide us, to teach us the values of responsibility, hard work, and respect for others.

3. Please, we beg of you, take the time to evaluate the progress our fathers have made, to see the genuine effort they are putting forth to become better men, better fathers.

4. Acknowledge the work they have done to address the root causes of their past mistakes, the steps they have taken to ensure they will never repeat those actions.

5. Recognize the future goals and plans our fathers have set for themselves, the dreams they have to rebuild the families they have torn apart.

6. Give them the chance to prove that they are worthy of our trust, that they can be the pillars of strength and support that every child deserves.

7. Understand that our fathers are not beyond redemption, that with the right guidance and opportunities, they can become the men we need them to be.

8. Empower them to take responsibility for their actions, to make amends, and to work tirelessly to regain our love and respect.

9. Provide them with the resources and support they need to reintegrate into our lives, to rebuild the bonds that have been broken.

To the Guardians of Freedom,

As the fatherless children, we come to you once again, this time with a plea that transcends the confines of our past appeals. We ask that you see our fathers, and our shared plight, through a different lens - one that illuminates the profound complexities and the glimmer of hope that lies within.

Our fathers are not merely criminals, but flawed human beings who have made grievous mistakes, often driven by a misguided sense of purpose and a desire to provide for and protect their families. They have lost sight of the true meaning of family, of the irreplaceable bond between a father and his child, as they grappled with the belief that their actions were necessary, even as they tore their families asunder.

Empathize with the internal struggles they have faced, the cognitive dissonance that has torn them apart. Recognize the remorse and the genuine desire for redemption that now burns within them, a flame that has been ignited by the realization of the harm they have caused and the gaping void they have left in our lives.

Understand that their absence has not only deprived us of their physical presence, but has also robbed us of the guidance, support, and unconditional love that only a father can provide. Imagine the weight of our broken hearts, the longing for the fathers we once knew, the men we still believe they can become, if only given the chance to prove their worthiness.

Envision the transformative potential that lies within our fathers, the opportunity for them to not only redeem themselves but to become the role models and pillars of strength that we so desperately need. Consider the broader societal impact that can be achieved by granting our fathers a second chance, as they emerge from incarceration armed with the tools and the determination to break the cycle of fatherlessness and create a future of hope and connection.

Ultimately, we ask that you view our fathers, and our shared plight, through the lens of compassion, understanding, and a belief in the power of redemption. For in doing so, you hold the key to reuniting us, the fatherless children, with the fathers we yearn to embrace once more.

We stand before you, not as accusers, but as advocates for a more just and empathetic approach to justice. Grant our fathers the freedom they seek, not as a matter of leniency, but as an investment in the future — a future where we, the fatherless children, can find solace in the embrace of the fathers we have always longed for.

Sincerely,

The Fatherless Children of the World

Chapter 5:
The Importance of Addressing Long-Neglected Mistakes

To the esteemed members of the Senate, Governor, and voters, It is imperative that we address the long-neglected mistakes and shortcomings in our current justice system. Every year, bills are proposed in an attempt to seek a lower percentage of time served by inmates, yet year after year, these proposals are shot down. The prevailing sentiment is that no hardened criminal deserves to be released, perpetuating a cycle of punishment without true rehabilitation.

But where does this leave the taxpayers who fund these correctional facilities and the programs that are meant to rehabilitate those within their walls? It is time for someone to step out of the shadows and speak up on behalf of these hard-earned dollars that are being allocated to a system that is failing those it claims to serve.

The truth is, the programs offered within these facilities are often inadequate and ineffective. There is a lack of focus on true rehabilitation and a dearth of resources dedicated to helping inmates address the root causes of their criminal behavior. Without a comprehensive approach to reform and rehabilitation, these individuals are left to languish within the system, perpetuating a cycle of incarceration and recidivism.

It is time to acknowledge that true rehabilitation is not only a moral imperative but also a practical necessity. By investing in programs that address the underlying issues that lead individuals down the path of crime, we can not only save taxpayer dollars in the long run but also create a more just and equitable society for all.

Let us work together to push for meaningful reform that prioritizes rehabilitation and reintegration for formerly incarcerated individuals. It is time to recognize that everyone deserves a second chance, and by addressing the mistakes of the past, we can pave the way for a brighter future for all.

Florida, like many other states, has experienced fluctuations in crime rates over the years. It is important for policymakers and law enforcement agencies to closely monitor these trends and take proactive measures to address any increase in crime.

From 2005 to 2023, it's facts that there have been fluctuations in major crime categories such as violent crime, property crime, and others. Factors such as economic conditions, changes in law enforcement practices, population growth, and social issues can all impact crime rates.

To address rising crime rates, it is crucial for communities to come together and support initiatives that focus on crime prevention, rehabilitation, and addressing root causes of criminal behavior. Investing in education, mental health resources, job training programs, and community policing can all help reduce crime and create safer neighborhoods.

It is also important for residents to be actively engaged in their communities, report suspicious activity, and work with law enforcement to ensure the safety and security of all residents.

Establishing Transition Houses for Rehabilitation and Reintegration in Florida

The state of Florida is in dire need of more transition houses to provide adult supervision and support for individuals who are ready to reintegrate into society after undergoing rehabilitation. Every day, we hear stories of men, both young and old, expressing their readiness to return home with reformed mindsets and a strong desire for a fresh start. By investing taxpayer dollars into establishing more transition houses, we can provide a crucial support system for these individuals as they navigate the challenging path of reintegration.

Transition houses offer a structured and supportive environment for individuals transitioning from a life of crime to one of rehabilitation and redemption. With professional supervision and guidance, residents of these houses can address their past behaviors, confront their issues, and work towards rebuilding their lives in a positive and productive manner.

The establishment of more transition houses across Florida will not only provide a safe and structured environment for individuals seeking a second chance but also help reduce recidivism rates by offering crucial support and resources for successful reintegration. By investing taxpayer dollars into these facilities, we can make a tangible impact on the lives of those in need and contribute to building a safer and more compassionate community.

In conclusion, the establishment of more transition houses in Florida holds immense potential to support individuals in their journey towards rehabilitation and reintegration. By investing taxpayer dollars into these facilities, we can provide a lifeline for those seeking a second chance and help pave the way for a brighter and more hopeful future. It is time to prioritize the well-being and success of our residents by expanding access to transition houses and ensuring that no one is left behind in their quest for redemption.

It is essential to acknowledge the challenges that individuals face when transitioning from prison back into society, especially after serving long periods of time. The routines and customs of prison can become ingrained in someone's behavior, making it difficult to readjust to life outside. This is why transition houses play a vital role in providing a structured environment for individuals to ease back into society, reconnect with their families, and rebuild their lives.

Non-violent offenders who have spent significant time in prison may struggle with the idea of reintegration, as the outside world can feel unfamiliar and overwhelming after years behind bars. Transition houses offer a supportive setting where individuals can receive guidance, counseling, and assistance in adjusting to life outside of prison.

By offering a safe and supportive space for individuals to transition back into society before completing their full sentence, transition houses help prevent the shock of sudden freedom and facilitate a smoother reentry process. This approach not only benefits the individuals themselves but also contributes to public safety by reducing the likelihood of recidivism.

Overall, the establishment of transition houses for individuals reentering society after long periods of incarceration is a crucial step in ensuring successful rehabilitation and reintegration. By providing the necessary support and resources, we can help individuals navigate the challenges of post-prison life and ultimately create a safer and more compassionate community for all.

Chapter 6:
Transforming Pain into Progress

As an inmate navigating the complexities of the prison system, it is all too easy to get lost in the sense of hopelessness and despair. The system, with its games and challenges, can easily overshadow any glimmer of progress or positivity. However, within the confines of a prison cell, there lies an opportunity to transform pain into progress and emerge as a stronger, more resilient individual.

While incarcerated, time becomes both a burden and a gift. It is a burden in the sense that every minute spent behind bars can feel like an eternity, a constant reminder of the mistakes and circumstances that led to incarceration. However, it is also a gift, offering a unique opportunity for self-reflection, growth, and transformation.

Many inmates are quick to succumb to the negativity and sense of futility that pervades the prison environment. It is easy to become jaded, to focus on the injustices of the system and to fall into a cycle of bitterness and apathy. However, there is another path—one that involves turning pain into progress, transforming challenges into opportunities, and emerging from the darkness of incarceration with a renewed sense of purpose and resilience.

One of the key ways to achieve this transformation is by shifting focus away from dwelling on the flaws of the system and towards self-improvement and growth. Despite the limitations and constraints of the prison system, there are opportunities for personal development and education that can be seized upon. Programs within the prison system offer a chance to acquire new skills, pursue education, and engage in meaningful activities that can foster personal growth and development.

However, for those facing life sentences, the question of hope and purpose can be particularly daunting. In the state of Florida, where the prospect of a life behind bars looms large, finding hope can seem like an impossible task. Yet, even in the face of such bleak circumstances, there is still room for hope and redemption.

Hope can be found in the small victories, the moments of connection with others, and the opportunities for self-improvement and growth. By focusing on personal progress, seeking out sources of inspiration and resilience, and refusing to be defined by the past, even those facing life sentences can find a sense of purpose and hope within the confines of a prison cell.

Transforming pain into progress is a journey that requires courage, determination, and a willingness to embrace change. By shifting perspective, focusing on personal growth, and finding hope in the midst of adversity, inmates can begin to rewrite their stories and emerge from the darkness of incarceration with a renewed sense of purpose, resilience, and possibility.

Finding Hope in the Shadows of Long-Term Sentences

The weight of a long-term sentence, compounded by habitual attachments that only serve to increase its duration, can cast a shadow of hopelessness and despair over even the most resilient of individuals. When the judge's gavel falls and the sentence is handed down, it can feel like the promise of hope has all but vanished, leaving behind a bleak landscape of uncertainty and unfulfilled dreams.

In the wake of a long-term sentence, the absence of anyone addressing the issues surrounding incarceration can only serve to deepen the sense of isolation and abandonment. As the ones who held the power to pass judgment disappear into the halls of justice, leaving behind a trail of shattered lives and broken dreams, the question of where to find hope becomes increasingly urgent and elusive.

The promise of hope, in the face of seemingly insurmountable odds, must come from within. It is a spark that flickers in the darkness of incarceration, a beacon of light that offers a glimmer of possibility amidst the shadows of despair. While the external world may offer little in the way of support or encouragement, the source of hope lies in the resilience, determination, and inner strength of the individual facing a long-term sentence.

For those navigating the complexities of the prison system, the path to finding hope begins with a refusal to succumb to the despair that threatens to engulf them. It is a conscious choice to resist the narrative of hopelessness and instead seek out opportunities for personal growth, self-improvement, and transformation.

While it may seem that the government's lack of funding for programs to provide a brighter future for incarcerated individuals is a significant barrier to progress, there is still room for hope within the confines of a prison cell. The financial constraints that limit the availability of resources and opportunities can be counteracted by a collective effort to create programs, initiatives, and support networks that empower individuals to embrace change and rewrite their stories.

In the absence of external support, the onus falls on those within the prison community to band together, support one another, and create pathways to hope and redemption. By teaching, mentoring, and developing programs that foster personal growth and transformation, individuals can break free from the constraints of their circumstances and forge a new path forward.

Finding hope in the shadows of long-term sentences is a challenging and arduous journey, but it is one that is essential for maintaining a sense of purpose, resilience, and possibility. By refusing to be defined by the length of their sentence or the limitations of the system, individuals can reclaim their agency, redefine their future, and discover that hope is not a distant dream but a tangible reality that can be found within the darkest of circumstances.

Chapter 7:
Building Bridges of Overstanding

I n the shadows of our long-term sentences, we find ourselves yearning for more than just surface-level understanding. We, the incarcerated, are tired of being seen through a lens of limited comprehension, especially when it comes to our growth, change, and desire to make right choices. We don't seek mere understanding; we seek overstanding - a deeper, more profound recognition of our struggles, aspirations, and potential.

We, the incarcerated, acknowledge the concerns and apprehensions that may arise when discussing the possibility of releasing individuals who have been labeled as murderers, robbers, thieves, or threats to society. We understand the fear and uncertainty that may grip the hearts of those who have never walked in our shoes, who only see us through the lens of our past mistakes. But we also believe in the power of transformation, redemption, and second chances.

To the government officials and policymakers who hold the key to our fate, we speak truth boldly. We understand the complexities of budget allocations and financial constraints, but we also see the irony in prioritizing funding for projects that do not directly benefit those within the walls of our institutions. The disparity between the resources allocated to infrastructure and the resources dedicated to rehabilitation is a stark reminder of the systemic injustices that plague our criminal justice system.

Let us shine a light on the everyday realities that we face behind bars. The sweltering heat that engulfs the institutions across Florida, where men live in fear for their lives, yearning for more fans or a reliable cooling system to provide relief. The exorbitant prices in the canteens, where items are marked up over 70% compared to society's prices, creating an additional burden on already strained finances.

And let us not overlook the issue of safety within these walls. Institutions secured by a greater number of untrained officers than certified ones, creating a volatile and unpredictable environment where violence and unrest can easily take root. How can we speak of rehabilitation and redemption when the very places meant to facilitate change are rife with danger and insecurity?

Building bridges of overstanding requires a willingness to listen, to empathize, and to engage in meaningful dialogue. It calls for a collective effort to address the systemic issues that perpetuate cycles of incarceration and hinder the prospects of redemption. It is a call to action for all parties involved - government officials, policymakers, law enforcement, and society at large - to recognize the humanity and potential within each individual behind bars, and to work towards a system that prioritizes rehabilitation, support, and transformation.

In the shadows of our long-term sentences, let us strive not just for understanding, but for overstanding - a shared recognition of our struggles, our hopes, and our capacity for change. Let us build bridges that transcend judgment, fear, and division, and pave the way for a future where redemption and second chances are not just ideals, but tangible realities for all.

Overstanding is better than an understanding. When trying to find a solution to correct something. Many government officials may quickly dismiss the concerns of the incarcerated as mere "tail talk." This is a common response when the dominant narrative is one of negativity and skepticism. However, it is crucial to understand the profound frustration felt by those who are earnestly striving for personal transformation and seeking to uplift their fellow brothers behind bars.

Contrasting Realities: The Media's Distortion

As you and your fellow inmates give it your all to change and help others in their journey of redemption, the outside world often remains oblivious to these uplifting endeavors. Every time you turn on the television, it is yet another reality show showcasing the true negative side of prison life. This stark contrast between the lived experiences of the incarcerated and the distorted depictions in the media is a source of deep anguish.

The Nuanced Landscape of Prison Life

In prison, just as in society at large, not everyone walks the path of righteousness. Yet, the nuanced realities of life behind bars are often overshadowed by sensationalized narratives. All sides of the story are known, and allowing everyone the right to choose who they deal with is crucial. However, the righteous stories of personal transformation and communal support are not being told or displayed throughout these TV reality shows.

The Untold Stories of Redemption

How many prison-focused reality shows actually take the time to highlight the men who have dedicated their lives to Yahweh, God, Allah, Jehovah, or any higher power of their choice? What platforms delve into the stories of those who tirelessly mentor their peers, helping young and old men alike to obtain their GED or embark on a transformative journey?

The "Dog and Pony Show" for Funding

This side of the story is only told when the authorities need to put on a convincing "dog and pony show." This typically occurs when the Department of Corrections seeks approval for a program grant, which rakes in millions of dollars annually. These funds, derived from taxpayers who themselves struggle to make ends meet, could be better utilized in bolstering the education system for our youth. If society truly believes that the incarcerated should remain "caged like dogs," then what is the true purpose of these programs?

The Perplexing Questions of the Incarcerated

This disconnect between the rhetoric and the reality raises a host of pertinent questions from the incarcerated population. Why are they being enrolled in business or parenting programs when they are serving life sentences? How can these programs possibly apply to individuals with no prospect of reintegrating into society? The underlying suspicion is that the primary motivations behind these initiatives are not rooted in genuine rehabilitation, but rather in financial gain and the maintenance of a flawed system.

Reasons for the Disconnect

There can be two possible reasons for this disconnect: 1) The authorities may genuinely see the change in the man as a whole, recognizing the value in nurturing personal growth, even if the individual may never reenter society. 2) They may be gaining a substantial amount of money from the various programs, with rehabilitation being a secondary consideration, if not an afterthought.

The Need for Authentic Rehabilitation

Ultimately, the core issue lies in the fact that all of this is being done without rehabilitation being the primary focus. The programs and initiatives, while seemingly designed to facilitate positive change, are often overshadowed by the pursuit of financial gain and the preservation of a system that thrives on the continued incarceration of individuals.

Bridging the Divide: A Call for Transparency and Accountability

The chapter delves deeper into the contrasting narratives, the marginalized stories of redemption, the staged "dog and pony show" performances, and the perplexing questions that arise from the incarcerated individuals themselves. This exploration aims to shed light on the multifaceted challenges and the urgent need to bridge the divide between the government's rhetoric and the lived experiences of those behind bars. Only through genuine transparency, accountability, and a genuine commitment to rehabilitation can the system truly serve the well-being of both the incarcerated and the broader society.

A Necessary Reckoning

As I sit alone in this dimly lit cell, my mind races with the sobering realities of life behind bars. I can't help but reflect on the narratives that have long dominated the public discourse surrounding incarceration, and a deep well of frustration bubbles within me.

I've lost count of the times I've heard government officials dismiss the concerns of the incarcerated as mere "tail talk," our words falling on deaf ears. It's a pattern of dismissal that has become all too familiar, a stubborn refusal to acknowledge the nuanced truths that lay beneath the surface.

My own story is a testament to the complexities of the criminal justice system, a tapestry woven with threads of trauma, desperation, and the relentless pursuit of redemption. As a young man, I made choices that landed me here, choices that have haunted me for years. Yet, within the confines of this institution, I've found a renewed sense of purpose, a determination to not only transform my own life but to uplift those around me.

If only they could see the men and women in here who are working tirelessly to better themselves, I think to myself, my eyes drifting towards the barred window. The ones who are finding solace in their faith, mentoring their peers, and striving to make amends for their past mistakes.

But the reality is that the world beyond these walls remains largely oblivious to these stories of resilience and redemption. The media, with its insatiable appetite for sensationalism, continues to bombard the public with the same narrow, negative depictions of prison life – a caricature that bears little resemblance to the complex realities I and my fellow inmates face day in and day out.

As I contemplate the deeper implications of this disconnect, a sense of urgency begins to take hold. I recognize that the dismissive rhetoric of officials and the distorted narratives in the media are not just a disservice to the incarcerated, but a threat to the very fabric of our communities.

If we can't even tell our own stories, how can we ever hope to create meaningful change? I whisper to myself, my fist clenching with determination.

It's in that moment that I know I can no longer remain silent. The time has come to shatter the walls of indifference, to demand that the world listen to the voices that have been marginalized for far too long. This is not about seeking sympathy or exposure, but about forging a path towards true accountability and rehabilitation – a future where the scourge of fatherless homes can be addressed at its very roots.

With a renewed sense of purpose, I begin to share my story, not just with my fellow inmates, but with anyone who will lend an open ear. I speak of the trauma that led me down a dangerous path, of the transformative power of faith and community, and of the unwavering determination that has sustained me during my darkest moments.

My words, once timid and hesitant, soon gain strength and conviction. I become a beacon of hope, rallying my peers to rise up and demand that our stories be heard, our truths be acknowledged, and our potential be nurtured – not just for our own sake, but for the sake of the generations to come.

As the days turn into weeks, my story begins to ripple outward, challenging the status quo and shattering the illusions that have long shrouded the criminal justice system. I know that the road ahead will be arduous, fraught with resistance and skepticism, but I am undaunted. For me, this is not just a personal crusade, but a necessary reckoning – a chance to pave the way for a future where the incarcerated can truly be seen as human beings worthy of dignity, redemption, and a second chance.

In the quiet moments, when the noise of the prison has faded and the weight of my circumstances threatens to overwhelm me, I close my eyes and envision a world where my story, and the stories of countless others like me, will be the catalysts for lasting, meaningful change. It's a vision that fuels my determination, a beacon of hope that will guide me through the darkest of times.

For me, this is not just a battle for my own freedom, but a fight for the future of my community, my family, and the generations that will come after me. And I am more than ready to take up the mantle, to be the voice that shatters the silence and ignites the spark of transformation.

Chapter 8:
Embracing Accountability and Change

As I sit down to write this chapter, I am reminded of the power that accountability holds in our lives. It can be a tough pill to swallow, accepting that we are responsible for our actions and their consequences. However, once we embrace this accountability, we open ourselves up to the possibility of change and growth.

I have come to understand that change is inevitable. It is a natural part of life, and it is up to us to either resist or embrace it. By taking ownership of our choices and behaviors, we pave the way for positive transformation.

Accountability, for me, is not about assigning blame or punishment. Instead, it is about taking a hard look at ourselves and acknowledging where we may have fallen short. It is about recognizing our mistakes, learning from them, and making the necessary adjustments to prevent them from happening again.

I have learned that true accountability requires courage and humility. It takes courage to face our shortcomings and acknowledge our faults. It takes humility to accept feedback and guidance from others, even when it is uncomfortable or challenging.

In my own journey towards accountability and change, I have discovered that it is not a solo endeavor. We cannot do it alone. We need the support and encouragement of others to hold us accountable and help us stay on track.

I have also realized that accountability is not a one-time commitment. It is an ongoing process that requires constant evaluation and reflection. We must be willing to adapt and evolve as we continue to grow and learn.

Change can be a scary and daunting prospect, but it is also necessary for personal development and fulfillment. It is through change that we uncover our true potential and discover the strength and resilience within us.

As I reflect on my own experiences, I am reminded of the times when I resisted change and avoided taking accountability for my actions. It only led to more pain and frustration. It was only when I embraced accountability and welcomed change that I was able to break free from old patterns and create a new path for myself.

In embracing accountability and change, I have learned to let go of fear and uncertainty. I have learned to trust in the process and believe in my ability to adapt and grow. I have learned that change is not something to be feared, but rather, something to be embraced with an open heart and mind.

So, I urge you to take a step back and reflect on your own journey towards accountability and change. Are there areas in your life where you may be avoiding responsibility? Are there opportunities for growth and development that you are overlooking? Embrace the challenge, embrace the change, and watch as your life transforms before your very eyes.

Yarah writes: "Members of the state of Florida, I stand here today to address the critical issue of accountability and how we can work together to create a better future for all. Accountability is not just a personal responsibility; it is a collective commitment that we must all uphold in order to ensure the well-being and prosperity of our state and its people.

As individuals, we must be willing to accept accountability for our actions and the impact they have on others. We must take ownership of our mistakes and shortcomings, and be open to feedback and guidance from those around us. This level of personal accountability is crucial for our own growth and development, as well as for the betterment of our communities and society as a whole.

But accountability is not just an individual endeavor. It is also a shared responsibility that requires the active participation and commitment of the state and its institutions. The state of Florida must also be willing to carry its fair share of accountability in order to create a more just and equitable society for all.

So, I pose this question to the state of Florida: What level of accountability are you willing to carry in order to create a brighter future for our state? Here are a few options that I believe could help us work towards a more accountable and prosperous future together:

- Option 1: Increase transparency and accountability within government institutions by implementing regular audits and public reports on actions and decisions made.

- Option 2: Invest in education and resources to promote accountability and ethical behavior across all levels of society, starting from schools and continuing into the workforce.

- Option 3: Establish clear guidelines and consequences for unethical or irresponsible behavior, both within government and in the private sector, to ensure accountability at all levels.

By considering these options and committing to a culture of accountability, we can create a state where trust, integrity, and responsibility are upheld by all. Let us work together to build a brighter future for Florida, where accountability is not just a buzzword, but a guiding principle that shapes our actions and decisions for the betterment of all."

Yarah's words hung in the air, as he awaited the response of the state representatives. He hoped that his message would resonate with them and pave the way for a more accountable and prosperous future for the state of Florida.

I sat amongst my fellow incarcerated brothers, feeling a sense of determination burning within me. I knew the potential that each of us held, despite our current circumstances. With a steady gaze and unwavering resolve, I began to speak, my voice filled with conviction.

"I know what my fellow incarcerated brothers, locked up like myself, can do if given a chance," I began, my words echoing through the room. "I have seen the positive impact that individuals like Mr. Ricky White and Mr. Dakota have made by coming back into the system and serving. Their dedication and commitment to making a difference, even after experiencing freedom, serves as an inspiration to all of us."

My words struck a chord with my fellow inmates, who listened attentively as I continued. "Their willingness to provide service wherever it is needed, their unwavering support and guidance - these are the qualities that we strive to embody. Each time they walk back through those gates after being free, it means a great deal to all of us. They are living proof that redemption is possible, that we can make a positive impact on the world around us."

As I spoke, my thoughts turned to my own child, a precious reminder of the stakes involved. "The impact I will cause in my child's life would be great for her," I stated confidently. "Our kids love us for as much as they know us. Society may look at us as the men we have become, but our children see beyond that. They see the love, the strength, and the potential within us. And it is our responsibility to live up to that potential, to show them what true redemption and transformation look like."

My words carried a weight of purpose and meaning, inspiring my fellow inmates to reflect on their own paths and the impact they could have on the world around them. As I concluded my speech, a sense of unity and determination filled the room, a shared commitment to be the change we wished to see in ourselves and in society.

My promises hung in the air, a reminder that despite the challenges and obstacles we faced, there was hope for a better future. With God Yahweh guiding our way and the examples of Mr. Ricky White and Mr. Dakota serving as beacons of inspiration, I and my fellow inmates stood ready to make a difference, both within the prison walls and beyond.

Chapter 9:
Seeds of hope for a better future

Honorable government officials, as I address you today, I am reminded of the profound experiences witnessed within the confines of our correctional facilities. As the sun ascends over the prison yard, illuminating the hope and anticipation pervading the air, I stand among my fellow incarcerated individuals, each embracing the potential for personal growth and societal impact.

In a poignant moment of unity and purpose, we gather to sow the "Seeds of Hope for a Better Future." Within the prison walls, we recognize the transformative power residing within each individual - not merely as prisoners, but as catalysts for change with the capacity to shape a more promising destiny.

Together, we delicately plant seeds symbolizing resilience and determination, fostering a sense of community and shared vision for a brighter tomorrow. Through the exchange of personal stories, dreams, and aspirations, we cultivate bonds that transcend our immediate circumstances, finding solace in our collective journey of growth and renewal.

This chapter, rich with interconnected narratives of redemption and transformation, symbolizes a chorus of voices advocating for a future defined by second chances and societal progress. As we gaze upon the fledgling garden of hope we've nurtured, we are emboldened by the promise of new beginnings and inclusive opportunities for all.

As the day wanes and we prepare to return to our confines, a newfound sense of purpose and determination guides our steps, illuminating the path towards a more equitable and hopeful future. The seeds we've planted today serve as beacons of possibility, lighting the way for personal evolution and positive societal change.

I urge you, esteemed officials, to consider the message woven within the "Seeds of Hope for a Better Future." Let it resonate beyond these prison walls, inspiring a collective commitment to redemption, transformation, and the unwavering belief in a brighter tomorrow for all. Our journey towards individual empowerment and societal betterment has only just commenced, fueled by the enduring promise of hope and the transformative power of renewal.

As I write this to you, Ladies and gentlemen, esteemed guests. I am reminded of the profound power we hold in our hands to shape the bridges that will connect us to a brighter tomorrow. Each decision we make, every brick we lay, is a testament to our shared journey towards a future of unity, compassion, and possibility.

In our relentless pursuit of progress and transformation, let us remember that the bridges we aim to construct are not mere physical structures but symbolic representations of our interconnectedness and shared humanity. As we embark on this journey together, let us do so with a sense of purpose and commitment to building a world where all are welcomed, valued, and uplifted.

As we look towards the horizon, envisioning the bridges that await us, let us do so with a shared sense of responsibility and hope. Let us recognize the power we hold to bridge divides, mend broken relationships, and forge new connections that transcend the boundaries of our individual experiences.

With humility and empathy, let us lay each brick with care and intention, knowing that our actions today have the potential to shape a future defined by inclusivity, understanding, and unity. Let us embrace this collective endeavor with open hearts and minds, knowing that the bridges we build today will guide us towards a tomorrow where we stand stronger together.

In our shared pursuit of a better tomorrow, may we find inspiration in the knowledge that the seeds we sow today will blossom into bridges of hope, connection, and possibility for generations to come. Together, let us embark on this journey with courage and determination, knowing that the bridges we cross tomorrow are a reflection of the strength, resilience, and beauty of our shared humanity.

As we walk this path together, side by side, hand in hand, let us remember that the bridges we build today are not just for us, but for all who will follow in our footsteps. With unwavering commitment and a steadfast belief in the power of unity, let us continue to lay the bricks that will shape a world where bridges of connection and understanding transcend all boundaries.

Thank you for joining me on this journey towards a future where our shared bridges lead us to a world of boundless opportunity, compassion, and love. Together, let us build a tomorrow that shines bright with the promise of unity, hope, and possibility.

The Power of Teamwork - Lessons from the 6-Time Michael Jordan Bulls, In the world of basketball, few teams have achieved the level of success and dominance as the 1990s Chicago Bulls led by the legendary Michael Jordan. Their six championships in eight years stand as a testament to the power of teamwork, dedication, and a shared vision. Just as the Bulls soared to greatness on the court, we too can learn valuable lessons from their journey that can guide us in our collective pursuit of building bridges towards a brighter future.

The Bulls dynasty was not built overnight. It was the result of years of hard work, sacrifice, and unwavering commitment to a common goal. From the coaching staff to the players, everyone understood their roles and responsibilities, working in harmony to overcome challenges and propel the team to unprecedented success. This level of cohesion and camaraderie is essential in any team, whether on the basketball court or in the pursuit of building bridges that connect us as individuals and communities.

One of the key lessons we can derive from the Bulls' success is the importance of leadership and mentorship. Michael Jordan, often hailed as one of the greatest basketball players of all time, not only elevated his own performance but also inspired and empowered his teammates to excel beyond their limits. His leadership on and off the court set the standard for professionalism, work ethic, and resilience, serving as a guiding light for the entire team. Similarly, in our quest to build bridges of unity and understanding, strong leadership and mentorship are crucial in inspiring others to join us on this transformative journey.

Another pivotal aspect of the Bulls' success was their relentless pursuit of excellence and continuous improvement. Despite their championship wins, the team never became complacent or rested on their laurels. They understood that greatness is not a destination but a journey, requiring constant innovation, adaptation, and a willingness to evolve. This growth mindset is essential as we work together to build bridges that bridge divides, foster inclusivity, and promote harmony in our communities and beyond.

Furthermore, the Bulls exemplified the power of resilience and perseverance in the face of adversity. They faced numerous challenges and setbacks throughout their journey, from injuries to fierce competition, yet they never wavered in their belief in themselves and their teammates. It is this unwavering resolve and determination that propelled them to overcome obstacles and emerge stronger, united in their pursuit of excellence. Similarly, as we encounter obstacles and hurdles in our quest to build bridges of connection and understanding, let us draw inspiration from the Bulls' resilience and stand firm in our commitment to creating a better tomorrow for all.

In conclusion, the legacy of the 6-time Michael Jordan Bulls serves as a beacon of inspiration and guidance for us as we strive to build bridges of unity, compassion, and possibility. Through teamwork, leadership, excellence, resilience, and perseverance, we can overcome challenges, transcend boundaries, and create a world where all are welcomed, valued, and uplifted. Just as the Bulls reached the pinnacle of success through their collective efforts, together, we too can forge a future defined by inclusivity, understanding, and unity. Let us embrace this shared journey with open hearts and minds, knowing that the bridges we build today will lead us towards a tomorrow filled with boundless opportunity, compassion, and love.

Chapter 10:
Reimagining Florida's Legacy

Florida, known for its beautiful beaches, diverse culture, and rich history, holds a unique place in the American landscape. However, beneath its surface lies a complex tapestry of stories, experiences, and perspectives that have often been overlooked or marginalized. In this chapter, we delve into the process of redefining and reimagining Florida's legacy, emphasizing the importance of creating a more inclusive, diverse, and equitable narrative that truly reflects the state's true identity and values.

Rediscovering Forgotten Voices:

One of the key aspects of reimagining Florida's legacy is the rediscovery of forgotten voices and narratives that have been silenced or overshadowed by dominant historical perspectives. By shedding light on the experiences of marginalized communities, such as Indigenous peoples, African Americans, Hispanic Americans, and other minority groups, we can gain a deeper understanding of Florida's true history and legacy. Through oral histories, archives, and community engagement, we can uncover hidden stories and perspectives that have been excluded from mainstream narratives.

Acknowledging Historical Injustices:

To create a more inclusive and equitable narrative of Florida's legacy, it is essential to acknowledge and address the historical injustices that have shaped the state's past. From the displacement of Indigenous peoples to the legacies of slavery, segregation, and discrimination,

Florida's history is fraught with complex and often painful chapters. By confronting these difficult truths and acknowledging the harm inflicted on marginalized communities, we can begin the process of healing and reconciliation.

Celebrating Diversity and Cultural Heritage:

Florida's legacy is deeply intertwined with its diverse population, made up of people from various cultural backgrounds, ethnicities, and traditions. Embracing this diversity and celebrating the cultural heritage of all Floridians is vital to creating a more inclusive and reflective narrative of the state's history. By recognizing the contributions of different communities to Florida's development and growth, we can build a more cohesive and united vision of the state's legacy.

Promoting Equity and Justice:

In reimagining Florida's legacy, it is crucial to promote equity and justice for all residents of the state. This requires a commitment to dismantling systemic barriers and inequalities that continue to impact marginalized communities. By advocating for policies and initiatives that ensure equal access to opportunities, resources, and representation, we can work towards a more equitable and just future for all Floridians. Additionally, addressing issues of social and economic disparities can help create a more balanced and inclusive narrative of Florida's legacy.

Educating and Engaging the Community:

Central to the process of reimagining Florida's legacy is educating and engaging the community in meaningful dialogue and reflection. By raising awareness about the state's diverse history, promoting dialogue around difficult topics, and fostering a sense of shared responsibility for shaping the state's legacy, we can cultivate a more informed and active citizenry. Through community-based initiatives, educational programs, and public forums, we can empower Floridians to actively participate in redefining and reshaping the state's narrative.

In the context of fatherless homes and the impact on children, the themes explored in Chapter 10 of reimagining Florida's legacy can have profound implications for addressing the challenges faced by children growing up without a father figure. By considering the power of language in shaping our identities and relationships, we can explore how fostering inclusivity, celebrating diversity, promoting equity, and engaging the community can play a crucial role in supporting children in fatherless homes and saving them from the negative effects of this absence.

1. Rediscovering Forgotten Voices:

In the case of children growing up in fatherless homes, their voices and experiences are often overlooked or marginalized within societal narratives. By shedding light on the stories and struggles of these children and acknowledging the unique challenges they face, we can provide a platform for their voices to be heard and their needs to be addressed. Through community engagement and support programs, we can empower these children to share their experiences and seek help when needed.

2. Acknowledging Historical Injustices:

The absence of a father figure in a child's life can stem from a variety of historical and systemic injustices, such as incarceration rates, economic disparities, or social norms. By acknowledging the root causes of fatherless homes and addressing the underlying issues that contribute to family breakdown, we can work towards creating a more equitable and just environment for children in need. This includes advocating for policies and resources that support at-risk families and provide opportunities for fathers to be actively involved in their children's lives.

3. Celebrating Diversity and Cultural Heritage:

Children in fatherless homes come from diverse backgrounds and cultural heritages, each with their unique strengths and challenges. By celebrating this diversity and recognizing the resilience and strength of these children, we can foster a sense of pride and belonging that transcends their family structure. Providing culturally responsive support services and resources that honor the backgrounds of these children can help build a sense of identity and connection that is essential for their well-being.

4. Promoting Equity and Justice:

Addressing the impact of fatherless homes on children requires a commitment to promoting equity and justice within our communities. This includes ensuring that all children, regardless of their family structure, have access to quality education, healthcare, and support services that meet their individual needs. By advocating for policies that address the social and economic disparities that contribute to family breakdown, we can create a more level playing field for children in fatherless homes and empower them to thrive despite their circumstances.

5. Educating and Engaging the Community:

Effective support for children in fatherless homes requires a community-wide effort to raise awareness and create a supportive network of resources. By educating the community about the challenges faced by these children and engaging them in meaningful dialogue and action, we can foster a sense of shared responsibility for their well-being. This can involve community-based initiatives, mentorship programs, support groups, and other resources that provide a safety net for children in need.

In summary, drawing parallels between the themes in this Chapter 10 and the challenges faced by children in fatherless homes can provide a roadmap for supporting these vulnerable individuals and saving them from the negative impacts of their circumstances. By embracing inclusivity, celebrating diversity, promoting equity and justice, and engaging the community in meaningful ways, we can create a more supportive and nurturing environment for children in fatherless homes to thrive and reach their full potential.

Overcoming Adversity

In the tapestry of life, challenges are the threads that weave together our experiences and shape our journey. These challenges come in various forms and sizes, testing our resolve and character along the way. It is in these moments of adversity that we are truly tested, where our true strength and resilience are revealed.

Challenges are not obstacles meant to hinder us, but rather opportunities for growth and development. They serve as stepping stones towards our goals, pushing us to go beyond our comfort zones and reach new heights. As we navigate through life's challenges, it is essential to cultivate a mindset of perseverance and determination, allowing us to overcome any obstacle that comes our way.

Resolve plays a crucial role in facing challenges head-on. It is the unwavering determination and commitment to persevere in the face of adversity. When obstacles arise, it is our resolve that keeps us grounded and focused on our goals. By staying true to our values and beliefs, we can navigate through challenges with grace and resilience, emerging stronger and more empowered than before.

Character is the foundation upon which we build our lives. It is the essence of who we are, our values, morals, and integrity. When faced with adversity, our true character is revealed, showcasing our strengths, weaknesses, and areas for growth. It is through overcoming challenges that we can strengthen our character, refine our values, and become the best version of ourselves.

Our response to adversity is a reflection of our inner strength and mindset. It is how we choose to approach challenges, whether with fear and doubt or with courage and determination. By adopting a positive and proactive mindset, we can transform obstacles into opportunities and setbacks into stepping stones towards success. Our response to adversity ultimately determines our ability to overcome challenges and achieve our goals.

Strength is forged in the fires of adversity. It is through facing and overcoming challenges that we discover the depth of our inner resilience and fortitude. Adversity has the power to shape us, mold us, and strengthen us in ways we never thought possible. It is in the moments of struggle and hardship that we find our true strength, rising above the challenges that seek to hold us back.

To propel forward towards our goals, we must embrace and overcome adversity. It is through facing challenges head-on that we grow, learn, and evolve. Adversity is not a roadblock but a catalyst for growth and transformation. By harnessing the power of challenges, we can propel ourselves towards our goals with renewed energy, determination, and purpose.

Goals serve as our guiding light through the storms of adversity. They give us direction, purpose, and motivation to keep moving forward, even in the face of challenges. By setting clear and achievable goals, we can navigate through adversity with a sense of clarity and focus, staying true to our vision and mission. Goals provide us with the roadmap to success, guiding us towards our dreams and aspirations.

In the style reminiscent of the renowned author who emphasizes personal growth and leadership development, it is evident that overcoming adversity is not just about-facing challenges, but about embracing them as opportunities for growth and transformation. By focusing on developing our resolve, character, and response to adversity, we can strengthen our inner core and propel ourselves towards our goals with unwavering determination and purpose. Adversity may test us, but it is through overcoming these challenges that we truly discover our potential and ability to thrive in the face of adversity.

Chapter 11:
Restoring the Fabric of Community

I n a society where change is often measured by the actions of individuals, the stories of incarcerated fathers who have transformed their lives and are now actively working to better their communities serve as shining examples of redemption and hope. These men, once confined within the walls of prison, have emerged as pillars of strength and sources of inspiration for those around them. Their journeys from darkness to light not only reflect personal growth and moral change but also highlight the transformative power of second chances and the importance of community support in the process of rehabilitation.

One such individual is Ricky White, a man who spent a significant portion of his life behind bars for his past mistakes. Despite the challenges he faced upon his release, Ricky refused to be defined by his past and instead chose to focus on rebuilding his life and giving back to the community that had once turned its back on him. Through his tireless efforts and unwavering commitment to making a positive impact, Ricky has become a beacon of hope for others who are struggling to find their way.

Dakota is another remarkable example of an incarcerated father who has made a moral change in life and is now dedicated to bettering the community. After serving his time, Dakota recognized the significance of personal responsibility and the importance of setting a positive example for his children and those around him. Through his involvement in community outreach programs and mentorship initiatives, Dakota has shown that transformation is possible, no matter how difficult the journey may be.

Elmo's story is one of resilience and perseverance in the face of adversity. As a former inmate who struggled with a history of criminal behavior, Elmo knew that he had to make a change in order to break the cycle of negativity that had consumed his life. Through his unwavering determination and commitment to self-improvement, Elmo has not only turned his own life around but has also become a source of inspiration for others who are seeking redemption and a second chance.

Pastor Jolly's journey is perhaps the most profound of all, as he not only overcame the challenges of incarceration but also found his calling in serving others and spreading positivity within the community. As a spiritual leader and mentor to many, Pastor Jolly has dedicated his life to helping those in need and offering guidance to those who are struggling to find their way. His unwavering faith and commitment to making a difference have inspired countless individuals to pursue their own paths to redemption and embrace the power of transformation.

Collectively, Ricky White, Dakota, Elmo, and Pastor Jolly represent a beacon of hope and a testament to the human capacity for change and growth. Their stories of redemption and resilience serve as reminders that no one is beyond redemption and that with the right support and determination, it is possible to overcome even the most challenging of circumstances. As these men continue to give back to their communities and inspire others to follow in their footsteps, they are not only restoring the fabric of community but also paving the way for a brighter and more hopeful future for all.

The Positive Impact of Releasing Rehabilitated Inmates on Taxpayer Dollars

The Florida Department of Corrections plays a crucial role in the state's operations, receiving a significant portion of state budget funding, primarily from taxpayers' dollars. With expenses related to housing, feeding, providing medical care, staffing, and maintaining facilities for inmates, the corrections system represents a substantial financial burden on the state.

The state's Department of Corrections budget for the 2020-2021 fiscal year stood at approximately $2.7 billion, funded primarily by state appropriations derived from various revenue sources, including taxpayers' dollars. This significant budget allocation highlights the immense cost associated with managing the corrections system and inmate population.

While high incarceration rates and prison expenditures are a reality for many states, there is an opportunity to explore alternative approaches that could positively impact taxpayers' dollars and the corrections system itself. One such approach involves the release of inmates who have shown remarkable transformation and rehabilitation during their time in prison.

Releasing inmates who have demonstrated genuine efforts toward personal growth, skill development, and behavioral change can lead to several benefits. Firstly, it can reduce the financial strain on the state's budget allocated to the Department of Corrections. By freeing up resources currently used for incarcerating these individuals, taxpayer dollars can be directed toward more cost-effective and sustainable solutions.

Moreover, releasing rehabilitated inmates can contribute to a reduction in recidivism rates. When individuals are provided with opportunities for education, vocational training, mental health support, and reintegration programs while incarcerated, they are better equipped to successfully reintegrate into society upon release. This, in turn, can lead to a decrease in future crime rates and related incarceration costs.

Additionally, releasing rehabilitated inmates fosters a sense of hope, redemption, and second chances within the criminal justice system. It highlights the potential for positive change and acknowledges that individuals can transform their lives given the right support and resources. This approach aligns with the principles of rehabilitation and restorative justice, emphasizing the importance of recognizing and nurturing the inherent dignity and potential of every individual. Releasing inmates who have demonstrated significant progress and rehabilitation during their time in prison can have far-reaching benefits for both taxpayers and the corrections system. By reallocating resources towards effective rehabilitation programs and supporting successful reentry into society, states like Florida have the opportunity to not only reduce financial burdens but also promote a more humane and effective approach to criminal justice. Through this approach, we can harness the power of redemption, transformation, and second chances to create a more just and equitable society.

Chapter 12
Nurturing Compassion and Unity

The ripples of mass incarceration extend far beyond the prison walls, profoundly affecting the fabric of communities across the nation. The absence of fathers, mothers, and primary caregivers due to imprisonment creates a cascading effect, leaving indelible marks on families, neighborhoods, and society as a whole.

One of the most immediate and devastating impacts is the erosion of family structure. Children raised without a parent present are more likely to experience emotional and behavioral difficulties, academic struggles, and involvement in the juvenile justice system. The loss of a parent's income can plunge families into poverty, leading to housing instability, food insecurity, and limited access to essential resources. Moreover, the stigma associated with incarceration can isolate families, hindering their ability to seek support and rebuild their lives.

Beyond the family unit, entire communities bear the brunt of mass incarceration. Neighborhoods with high incarceration rates often grapple with concentrated poverty, unemployment, and crime. The absence of productive members of society can lead to a decline in economic activity, as well as a loss of social capital and community cohesion. Additionally, the disproportionate impact of incarceration on communities of color exacerbates existing racial disparities, perpetuating cycles of poverty and marginalization.

The criminal justice system's focus on punishment rather than rehabilitation has further compounded these issues. By removing individuals from their communities for extended periods, prisons often become training grounds for criminal behavior rather than places of reform. Upon release, former inmates often return to communities ill-equipped to reintegrate, facing significant barriers to employment, housing, and education. This can lead to recidivism, further destabilizing neighborhoods and reinforcing the cycle of incarceration.

Florida, a state synonymous with sunshine and tourism, also grapples with a significant challenge: reintegrating its vast population of returning citizens. With one of the highest incarceration rates in the nation, the Sunshine State has a particular responsibility to ensure that individuals reentering society have the support and opportunities needed to successfully transition back into their communities.

The economic implications of neglecting reintegration are substantial. Florida's workforce is constantly evolving, and former inmates represent a potential pool of skilled labor. Studies have shown that investing in reentry programs yields a positive return on investment by reducing recidivism rates and increasing employment. When ex-offenders are able to find stable employment, they contribute to the state's tax base and reduce the burden on social safety nets.

Moreover, reintegration is crucial for public safety. Individuals who successfully transition back into society are less likely to commit new crimes. By providing returning citizens with the necessary support and resources, Florida can create safer communities for everyone. Research indicates that states with effective reentry programs experience lower crime rates.

Finally, reintegration is a matter of social justice. Many individuals who become incarcerated are from marginalized communities already facing significant challenges. By providing opportunities for rehabilitation and reentry, Florida can help to break the cycle of poverty and crime that disproportionately affects these communities.

Florida's vibrant and diverse communities are essential to the successful reintegration of its returning citizens. Creating an environment where ex-offenders feel welcomed and supported is crucial to preventing recidivism and fostering a safer, more inclusive society.

One key aspect of building supportive communities is addressing the issue of housing. Many ex-offenders face significant challenges finding affordable and safe housing, often due to discriminatory housing practices and landlord prejudices. Programs like the Florida Housing Finance Corporation's Hard-to-House initiative aim to address this issue by providing rental assistance and housing counseling to individuals with barriers to housing.

Additionally, fostering strong partnerships between government agencies, community organizations, and the private sector is essential. Initiatives such as the Second Chance Act have provided funding for reentry programs in Florida, but more collaboration is needed. For example, the Tampa Bay Reentry Coalition brings together various stakeholders to address the complex needs of returning citizens.

Furthermore, addressing the stigma associated with incarceration is vital. Community-based organizations can play a pivotal role in changing public perceptions by offering education and awareness programs. Initiatives like the Florida Expungement Clinic, which assists individuals in clearing their criminal records, can also help to reduce stigma and create opportunities for ex-offenders.

Ultimately, building supportive communities requires a comprehensive approach that addresses the multifaceted challenges faced by returning citizens. By investing in housing, employment, education, and mental health services, Florida can create a more welcoming environment for ex-offenders and reduce the likelihood of recidivism.

Florida boasts a diverse landscape, with metropolitan areas experiencing significantly higher incarceration rates than rural regions. These disparities necessitate tailored strategies. Communities like Miami-Dade, Broward, and Orange Counties, for instance, grapple with disproportionately high rates of incarceration, often concentrated in specific neighborhoods.

A prime example is Miami-Dade County's Overtown neighborhood, historically marginalized and burdened by high crime rates. Initiatives like the Overtown Redevelopment Plan seek to revitalize the community through economic development, housing, and education programs. By addressing the root causes of crime, such as poverty and lack of opportunity, these efforts aim to reduce recidivism and create a more supportive environment for returning citizens.

Another challenge faced by these communities is the concentration of reentry resources. While some areas may have a plethora of programs, others may lack essential services. To address this imbalance, it is crucial to distribute resources equitably and ensure that communities with the highest need receive adequate support.

Moreover, collaboration between local governments, law enforcement agencies, and community-based organizations is essential. For instance, the Orlando Police Department's Community Policing Initiative has fostered positive relationships between law enforcement and residents in high-crime neighborhoods. By building trust and addressing community concerns, such initiatives can create a more welcoming environment for returning citizens.

Ultimately, addressing the specific challenges faced by communities with high incarceration rates requires a multifaceted approach. By investing in education, job training, affordable housing, and crime prevention strategies, Florida can create opportunities for its residents and reduce the likelihood of recidivism.

Effective community-based reentry programs are essential for supporting individuals transitioning from incarceration back into society. Florida has implemented various initiatives to address this challenge, and several strategies have proven successful.

Employment and Job Training

One of the most critical factors in successful reentry is employment. Programs like Florida's CareerSource centers offer job training, placement assistance, and support services to help ex-offenders find stable employment. Additionally, initiatives such as the Second Chance Act have funded employment programs specifically targeting returning citizens.

Housing and Stability

Access to affordable housing is a significant barrier for many reentering individuals. Programs like the Florida Housing Finance Corporation's Hard-to-House initiative provide rental assistance and housing counseling. Furthermore, partnerships between housing providers and reentry organizations can help to create supportive housing environments.

Mental Health and Substance Abuse Treatment

Addressing mental health and substance abuse issues is crucial for successful reentry. Florida has expanded access to treatment services through initiatives like the Florida Recovery Program. Community-based organizations also play a vital role in providing peer support and recovery services.

Education and Skill Development

Educational opportunities can empower returning citizens and increase their employability. Florida's adult education programs offer a pathway to obtaining a GED or high school diploma. Additionally, vocational training programs can equip individuals with the skills needed to succeed in the workforce.

Community Engagement and Support

Building strong relationships between returning citizens and their communities is essential for long-term success. Mentoring programs, volunteer opportunities, and community-based support groups can help individuals reintegrate and rebuild their lives.

Policy Reform

To create a more supportive environment for reentry, policy changes are necessary. Efforts to reduce barriers to employment, housing, and education for individuals with criminal records are essential. Florida has made progress in this area with expungement reforms and other policy changes, but more work is needed.

By implementing these strategies and fostering strong partnerships between government agencies, community organizations, and the private sector, Florida can create a more supportive environment for returning citizens and reduce recidivism rates.

Chapter 13:
Crafting a New Narrative

The pervasive stereotypes surrounding incarcerated individuals pose a significant barrier to their successful reintegration into society.[1]

Often labeled as criminals or threats, these individuals face prejudice and discrimination that limit their opportunities for employment, housing, and education.[2]

For instance, a study by the Vera Institute of Justice found that people with criminal records are less likely to be called back for job interviews compared to those without, even when controlling for factors like education and work experience. This disparity highlights the deep-seated biases that persist against formerly incarcerated individuals.

Moreover, these stereotypes can lead to the creation of a self-fulfilling prophecy. When individuals are constantly viewed through a negative lens, they are more likely to internalize these stereotypes, impacting their self-esteem and motivation. This can hinder their ability to overcome challenges and achieve their goals.

To address these issues, it is essential to challenge harmful stereotypes through education, awareness campaigns, and media representation. By humanizing the experiences of incarcerated

---

[1] An Exploration of Barriers to Offender Reintegration: Probation and Prison Officer Opinions Vs. Public Opinion by S M Nazmuz Sakib https://www.crimrxiv.com
[2] Expanding Economic Opportunity for Formerly Incarcerated Persons by The White House https://www.whitehouse.gov/cea

individuals and highlighting their potential for positive change, we can shift public perception and create a more inclusive society.

To bridge the divide between incarcerated individuals, their families, and the community, fostering empathy and understanding is paramount. By humanizing the experiences of those affected by incarceration, we can challenge preconceived notions and create a more compassionate society.

One powerful way to cultivate empathy is through storytelling. Sharing personal narratives of incarcerated individuals and their families can help to break down stereotypes and create a sense of connection. Initiatives like the Inside-Out Prison Exchange Program, where college students take classes inside prisons, facilitate dialogue and promote mutual understanding.

Furthermore, educational programs can play a vital role in fostering empathy. By teaching about the causes and consequences of crime, as well as the challenges faced by incarcerated individuals and their families, we can equip people with the knowledge and tools to build empathy.

For example, the Osborne Association in New York offers a variety of programs that focus on building empathy and understanding between incarcerated individuals and the community. Their Inside/Out program brings together incarcerated individuals and college students to engage in dialogue and learn from each other's experiences.

Establishing strong connections between incarcerated individuals, their families, and the broader community is essential for successful reintegration. Several practical steps can be implemented to foster these relationships:

Family Visitation and Support Programs

Regular and meaningful family visits are crucial for maintaining strong family bonds. Programs that facilitate these visits, such as video conferencing or extended visitation hours, can significantly impact the well-being of both incarcerated individuals and their families. Additionally, support groups for families of incarcerated individuals can provide a valuable outlet for sharing experiences and coping strategies.

Community-Based Reentry Programs

Collaborations between correctional facilities and community organizations can create seamless transitions for individuals returning home. Programs that offer housing assistance, job training, and mentorship can provide the necessary support for successful reintegration. For example, the Osborne Association in New York operates a variety of reentry programs that connect formerly incarcerated individuals with employment opportunities and community resources.

Restorative Justice Initiatives

Involving victims, offenders, and community members in the restorative justice process can foster healing and reconciliation. Programs that facilitate dialogue and reparation can help to rebuild trust and create a sense of shared responsibility for community safety.

Volunteer and Mentorship Programs

Matching incarcerated individuals with mentors from the community can provide guidance, support, and role models. Volunteer programs that involve community members in prison-based activities can also help to break down stereotypes and build bridges.

Education and Awareness Campaigns

Educating the public about the challenges faced by incarcerated individuals and their families can help to reduce stigma and promote empathy. Community events, workshops, and media campaigns can be used to raise awareness and encourage support.

By implementing these practical steps, communities can create a more welcoming environment for returning citizens and foster stronger bonds between incarcerated individuals, their families, and the broader community.

Community-led initiatives have proven to be instrumental in bridging the gap between incarcerated individuals, their families, and the wider community. These programs often demonstrate remarkable resilience and innovation in addressing the challenges faced by returning citizens.

The Osborne Association, New York

The Osborne Association is a prime example of a community-based organization making a significant impact. With a rich history dating back to 1933, the organization offers a wide range of programs aimed at reducing crime, recidivism, and victimization. Their Inside/Out program, which brings together incarcerated individuals and college students, has been particularly successful in fostering empathy and understanding. By creating opportunities for dialogue and shared learning, the program challenges stereotypes and builds bridges between different segments of society.

Philadelphia's Reentry Court

Philadelphia's Reentry Court is a specialized court designed to support individuals transitioning from prison back into the community. The court works closely with community partners to provide a comprehensive range of services, including housing, employment, and substance abuse treatment. By offering individualized attention and support, the Reentry Court has demonstrated success in reducing recidivism rates and improving the lives of returning citizens.[3]

San Francisco's Delancey Street Foundation

Delancey Street Foundation is a non-profit organization that provides comprehensive support services to individuals recovering from addiction and incarceration. Through a residential program that emphasizes self-sufficiency and personal responsibility, the foundation has helped countless individuals rebuild their lives. By offering employment opportunities within their own businesses, Delancey Street provides a stable foundation for former offenders to reintegrate into society.[4]

The Second Chance Act

While not strictly a community-led initiative, the Second Chance Act has provided significant funding for community-based reentry programs across the United States, including Florida. By supporting a wide range of services, such as employment training, housing

---

[3] https://www.youtube.com/watch?v=UeIrO8yPttA

[4] Delancey Street Foundation - Home www.delanceystreetfoundation.org

assistance, and substance abuse treatment, the Act has empowered communities to develop effective reentry strategies.[5]

The Role of Faith-Based Organizations

Faith-based organizations have been instrumental in providing support and resources to incarcerated individuals and their families. Many churches, synagogues, and mosques offer programs that focus on spiritual guidance, mentorship, and reintegration services. For example, the Prison Fellowship Ministry has a strong presence in many states, providing support to incarcerated individuals and their families through faith-based programs.[6]

These case studies demonstrate the power of community-led initiatives in addressing the challenges faced by returning citizens. By focusing on empathy, support, and collaboration, these programs have achieved remarkable success in helping individuals rebuild their lives and contribute positively to their communities.

---

[5] Community-Based Reentry Program (FY 2023)
www.nationalreentryresourcecenter.org
[6] Impacts of the Second Chance Act | Office of Justice Programs www.ojp.gov

Chapter 14:
Healing Wounds, Restoring Wholeness

T he current discourse surrounding incarceration often paints a bleak and one-sided picture, focusing on punishment rather than rehabilitation, and stigma rather than redemption. To truly reform our justice system and the lives of those affected, it is essential to reframe the conversation around incarceration. This begins with shifting the narrative from one of condemnation to one of potential, where the emphasis is placed on the humanity of the incarcerated and their capacity for change.

Historically, the language used in discussions about incarceration has been heavily laden with negative connotations. Words like "criminal," "inmate," and "offender" serve to dehumanize individuals, reducing them to the worst moments of their lives. To change this, we must adopt language that acknowledges the complexities of human behavior and the potential for growth. Referring to incarcerated individuals as "returning citizens" or "incarcerated fathers" is a small but powerful step in reshaping public perception. This shift in language helps to restore dignity and opens the door for society to see these individuals as more than their past mistakes.

Moreover, reframing the conversation involves highlighting the stories of transformation and redemption that often go untold. The narrative of incarceration should include the countless examples of men who, despite the harsh conditions of prison life, have used their time behind bars to educate themselves, mentor others, and prepare for a positive reentry into society. These stories of perseverance and self-improvement are vital in challenging the dominant narrative that incarceration is synonymous with failure. By focusing on these success stories, we can inspire hope and advocate for policies that support rehabilitation over retribution.

Reframing the conversation also means involving the voices of the incarcerated in the discussion. Too often, the people most affected by the criminal justice system are excluded from the conversations about its reform. Empowering incarcerated fathers to share their experiences and insights allows them to take ownership of their narratives and contributes to a more balanced and just discourse. These voices can provide invaluable perspectives on the challenges and successes of rehabilitation, offering a powerful counter-narrative to the notion that incarceration is an end rather than a beginning.

Promoting positive stories of redemption is essential in reshaping the public perception of incarceration and the individuals affected by it. For too long, the narrative around those who have been incarcerated has been dominated by tales of failure, recidivism, and the perceived dangers they pose to society. While these aspects cannot be ignored, they are only part of the story. Equally important, if not more so, are the stories of transformation and redemption that highlight the resilience, growth, and renewed purpose of those who have spent time behind bars.

Positive stories of redemption have the power to challenge the stereotypes that often define public understanding of incarcerated individuals. These stories illustrate that people are capable of profound change, even in the most difficult circumstances. By focusing on the journeys of those who have turned their lives around—often against tremendous odds—we can offer a more balanced view of what it means to be incarcerated and what it means to be free. These narratives serve as powerful tools for humanizing the incarcerated, reminding society that these individuals are not just statistics or case numbers, but real people with dreams, struggles, and the capacity for change.

One effective way to promote these stories is through the media. Documentaries, news stories, podcasts, and social media platforms can all play a role in amplifying the voices of those who have successfully rehabilitated. Media outlets often gravitate toward sensationalism, but by partnering with organizations that focus on criminal justice reform and rehabilitation, it is possible to create content that tells these redemption stories compellingly and authentically. These stories not only inform the public but also inspire other incarcerated individuals to believe that change is possible for them as well.

Education and community programs are also vital in promoting positive stories of redemption. Schools, churches, and community centers can serve as platforms for formerly incarcerated individuals to share their stories. These personal testimonies can be incredibly powerful, offering firsthand insights into the challenges and triumphs of rebuilding one's life after incarceration. Moreover, these stories can help dismantle the stigma that surrounds formerly incarcerated individuals, making it easier for them to reintegrate into society and contribute positively to their communities.

Promoting stories of redemption also requires active participation from policymakers and community leaders. When those in positions of power acknowledge and celebrate the successes of rehabilitated individuals, it sends a strong message that redemption is possible and valued. This can lead to the implementation of more supportive policies, such as increased access to education and job training for the incarcerated, as well as greater opportunities for reentry and reintegration. By recognizing and uplifting these positive stories, society can move toward a more compassionate and effective approach to criminal justice.

Empowering incarcerated fathers to share their voices is a crucial step toward transforming both the criminal justice system and the lives of those affected by it. When these men are given the platform to express their experiences, challenges, and aspirations, it not only aids in their personal growth but also educates the broader community, policymakers, and stakeholders about the true complexities of incarceration and the potential for meaningful change. This empowerment can lead to positive change within the prison system, in their families, and in society at large.

One of the primary ways to empower incarcerated fathers is through the creation and support of platforms that allow them to express themselves. Programs that focus on writing, public speaking, and the arts have proven to be effective tools for incarcerated individuals to articulate their experiences and emotions.

In addition to writing and the arts, programs that facilitate direct communication between incarcerated fathers and their families are also essential. Video calls, recorded messages, and in-person visits (where possible) allow these fathers to maintain relationships with their children and participate in their upbringing, even from behind bars. These interactions are not only beneficial for the children, who often suffer from the absence of their fathers but also for the fathers themselves, as they reinforce their roles as caregivers and providers. Such programs highlight the importance of maintaining family bonds during incarceration, which can significantly improve outcomes for both incarcerated individuals and their families.

A real-life example of this empowerment is the story of *Anthony Ray* Hinton, a man who spent 30 years on death row in Alabama for a crime he did not commit. During his time in prison, Hinton became a powerful advocate for other inmates, sharing his experiences and speaking out against the injustices of the system. After his exoneration, Hinton wrote a memoir titled *The Sun Does Shine*[7], in which he not only recounts his ordeal but also speaks about the importance of forgiveness, hope, and the power of one's voice.

───────────────────

[7] Hinton, Anthony Ray. "The Sun Does Shine." (2019). The book is New York Times Bestseller and winner of the 2019 Moore prize

His story has inspired countless others and has brought attention to the need for reform within the criminal justice system.

Another real-life example of this empowerment is the work of *Shaka Senghor*, a former inmate who transformed his life through writing and advocacy. While incarcerated, Senghor authored Writing *My Wrongs: Life, Death, and Redemption in an American Prison*, a memoir that details his journey from a troubled youth to a thoughtful, reform-minded individual. His book not only provided him with a means to process his past but also resonated with a wide audience, highlighting the potential for personal transformation within the prison system. Senghor's story has inspired many and brought attention to the importance of rehabilitation over mere punishment (Senghor, 2012).[8]

In Florida, similar initiatives can significantly impact incarcerated fathers. Programs like the Florida Department of Corrections' arts and education initiatives offer opportunities for inmates to engage in creative expression and storytelling. These programs enable fathers to document their lives, share their insights, and connect with their families and communities in meaningful ways. By participating in these initiatives, incarcerated men can break the cycle of stigma and isolation, fostering a sense of purpose and hope that is crucial for successful reintegration into society.

Moreover, empowering incarcerated fathers to share their voices involves leveraging digital platforms and media partnerships. Collaborations with organizations that focus on criminal justice reform can amplify these stories, reaching a broader audience and influencing public perception. For instance, initiatives like TEDxPrison events allow inmates to present their ideas and experiences to a wider audience, fostering dialogue and

---

[8] Senghor, S. (2012). Writing My Wrongs: Life, Death, and Redemption in an American Prison. Thomas Nelson.

understanding. These platforms not only validate the voices of incarcerated individuals but also challenge societal prejudices, promoting a more nuanced view of incarceration.

Empowering incarcerated fathers to share their voices also plays a critical role in shaping policy and advocacy efforts. When policymakers hear firsthand accounts of the struggles and successes of incarcerated individuals, it can inform more effective and humane legislation. This direct input ensures that reforms are grounded in the lived experiences of those most affected by the criminal justice system, leading to policies that prioritize rehabilitation, mental health support, and family reunification.

Media literacy and advocacy strategies are critical components in reshaping public perception of incarceration and advocating for the rights and dignity of incarcerated individuals, particularly fathers. In a society where media has a profound influence on shaping opinions and driving policy, understanding how to navigate and utilize media effectively is essential for both incarcerated individuals and those working to support them.

Media literacy involves the ability to access, analyze, evaluate, and create media in various forms. For incarcerated fathers and their advocates, media literacy is crucial for understanding how narratives about incarceration are constructed and disseminated. Often, media coverage of criminal justice issues is skewed toward sensationalism, focusing on crime and punishment rather than rehabilitation and redemption. This can perpetuate negative stereotypes and hinder efforts to reform the justice system.

By enhancing media literacy, incarcerated fathers can become more discerning consumers of media, recognizing biases, questioning sources, and understanding the broader context in which information is presented. This awareness is the first step toward countering harmful narratives and promoting more balanced and positive stories about those affected by the criminal justice system.

Effective advocacy strategies require a comprehensive understanding of the media landscape and the ability to craft compelling messages that resonate with both the public and policymakers. Advocacy efforts must be grounded in a clear understanding of the issues at hand and the goals of the movement. For incarcerated fathers, these goals often include advocating for fair treatment, access to rehabilitative programs, and opportunities for reintegration into society.

One effective advocacy strategy is the use of storytelling, which humanizes the issues and makes them relatable to a broader audience. Personal stories of incarcerated fathers—highlighting their challenges, growth, and desire for redemption—can be powerful tools in changing public perception. These stories can be shared through various media outlets, including social media, blogs, podcasts, and traditional news platforms. When these narratives are presented in a way that emphasizes common humanity and the potential for positive change, they can shift the focus from punishment to rehabilitation.

Advocates and incarcerated fathers themselves can engage directly with media professionals to ensure that their stories are told accurately and compassionately. This can involve writing op-eds, participating in interviews, or collaborating on documentary projects. By taking an active role in shaping how their stories are told, incarcerated fathers can challenge the dominant narratives that often marginalize them and instead present themselves as agents of change.

Furthermore, training incarcerated fathers in media communication skills can empower them to become advocates for themselves and their peers. Workshops on public speaking, writing, and media engagement can provide these men with the tools they need to effectively share their experiences and insights with the public. This not only benefits their personal development but also contributes to broader advocacy efforts aimed at reforming the criminal justice system.

The rise of digital and social media platforms has democratized the dissemination of information, making it easier for marginalized voices to reach a wide audience. Advocates can use these platforms to amplify the voices of incarcerated fathers, sharing their stories, insights, and calls for reform. Social media campaigns, online petitions, and virtual events can mobilize public support and put pressure on policymakers to address the issues facing incarcerated individuals.

For example, campaigns like #Cut50, which focuses on reducing the prison population, have successfully used social media to raise awareness, engage supporters, and influence policy discussions. By employing similar strategies, advocates for incarcerated fathers can build momentum for change and ensure that their voices are heard in the public arena.

empowering incarcerated fathers to share their voices is essential for creating a more just and empathetic society. By providing platforms for expression, supporting educational and creative programs, and fostering media partnerships, we can ensure that these men are not forgotten but are instead recognized as integral contributors to the narrative of redemption and societal improvement. Their stories of resilience and transformation can inspire change, promote understanding, and ultimately contribute to a more effective and humane criminal justice system.

Chapter 15:
Honoring the Journey Towards Reconciliation

The mental health crisis in prisons is a profound and pressing issue that impacts not only the incarcerated individuals themselves but also their families, communities, and society at large. Prisons, originally designed as institutions for punishment and deterrence, are increasingly being populated by individuals with severe mental health issues. This has turned many correctional facilities into de facto mental health institutions, often without the resources or training necessary to provide appropriate care.

The prevalence of mental health disorders among the incarcerated population is alarmingly high. Studies indicate that a significant percentage of inmates suffer from conditions such as depression, anxiety, bipolar disorder, schizophrenia, and post-traumatic stress disorder (PTSD). According to a report by the Bureau of Justice Statistics, nearly 37% of state and federal prisoners and 44% of jail inmates have been diagnosed with a mental health condition (Bureau of Justice Statistics, 2017).

The causes of this crisis are multifaceted. Many individuals with mental health disorders end up in prison due to a lack of access to adequate mental health care in the community. In many cases, their untreated or inadequately managed conditions contribute to behaviors that lead to incarceration. Moreover, the stress and trauma of the prison environment often exacerbate existing mental health issues or trigger new ones. The lack of appropriate mental health care and the harsh conditions within prisons can worsen symptoms, leading to a cycle of deterioration that is difficult to break.

One of the primary challenges in addressing the mental health crisis in prisons is the lack of adequate resources. Many correctional facilities are ill-equipped to handle the complex needs of inmates with mental health disorders. There is often a shortage of trained mental health professionals, including psychologists, psychiatrists, and counselors, resulting in inadequate treatment and support for those who need it most. Additionally, the focus on security and discipline within prisons can overshadow the need for compassionate care, leading to environments that are not conducive to mental health recovery.

The stigma associated with mental illness also plays a significant role in the crisis. Inmates with mental health disorders may be reluctant to seek help due to fear of being labeled or mistreated by both staff and fellow inmates. This stigma can lead to underreporting of mental health issues and further isolation of those who are suffering. Furthermore, the punitive nature of the prison system often means that behaviors associated with mental illness, such as self-harm or outbursts, are met with disciplinary action rather than appropriate medical intervention.

Impact on Incarcerated Fathers

The mental health crisis in prisons has a particularly devastating impact on incarcerated fathers. These men are often struggling with the dual burden of coping with their mental health issues while dealing with the emotional toll of being separated from their children and families. The stress of incarceration, compounded by untreated or poorly managed mental health conditions, can lead to a breakdown in family relationships and contribute to the cycle of trauma and dysfunction that is passed down through generations.

Incarcerated fathers with mental health issues may find it difficult to maintain regular communication with their children or participate in programs designed to strengthen family bonds. This can lead to feelings of guilt, shame, and hopelessness, further exacerbating their mental health struggles. Without proper support, these fathers may leave prison with even more severe mental health challenges, making it difficult for them to reintegrate into society and fulfill their roles as parents.

Addressing the mental health crisis in prisons requires a comprehensive and multifaceted approach. This includes increasing access to mental health care within correctional facilities, providing training for staff to recognize and respond to mental health issues, and integrating mental health services into reentry programs to support individuals as they transition back into the community. Moreover, it is essential to adopt a trauma-informed approach to care that recognizes the impact of past trauma on current mental health and behavior, and that seeks to provide healing rather than punishment.

To make meaningful progress, it is also necessary to challenge the broader societal issues that contribute to the mental health crisis in prisons, such as the criminalization of mental illness and the lack of community-based mental health services. By addressing these root causes, we can reduce the number of individuals with mental health disorders who end up in the criminal justice system and ensure that those who are incarcerated receive the care and support they need to heal and rebuild their lives.

Trauma-informed care is a crucial approach in addressing the mental health needs of incarcerated individuals, particularly within the prison system where many have experienced significant trauma both prior to and during their incarceration. This approach is not just beneficial—it is essential for fostering rehabilitation, reducing recidivism, and ultimately restoring the lives of those who have been deeply affected by traumatic experiences.

Understanding Trauma and Its Impact

Trauma can stem from various sources, including physical, emotional, and sexual abuse, domestic violence, substance abuse, loss of loved ones, and chronic exposure to violence or neglect. For many incarcerated individuals, these traumatic experiences began long before they entered the prison system. Studies show that a significant portion of the prison population has a history of childhood trauma, which often contributes to behaviors that lead to incarceration. The experience of being incarcerated itself can be traumatizing, exacerbating pre-existing mental health conditions and creating new ones.

Trauma affects the brain and body in profound ways, often leading to hypervigilance, emotional dysregulation, and difficulty trusting others. These responses can manifest in behaviors that are often misunderstood or punished within the prison environment. Without proper care, these behaviors can lead to a cycle of re-traumatization, where the prison experience perpetuates the very conditions that contributed to the individual's incarceration in the first place.

Trauma-informed care is an approach that acknowledges the pervasive impact of trauma and seeks to create a supportive environment that promotes healing and recovery. It is built on key principles that include safety, trustworthiness, peer support, collaboration, empowerment, and cultural sensitivity. These principles are designed to help individuals feel secure, valued, and understood, which are critical components in the healing process.

- **Safety:** Ensuring physical and emotional safety is the foundation of trauma-informed care. In a prison setting, this means creating an environment where individuals are protected from further harm, both from others and from themselves. It also involves establishing predictable routines and clear boundaries to help individuals regain a sense of control.

- **Trustworthiness and Transparency:** Building trust between incarcerated individuals and staff is essential. This can be achieved through open communication, consistent actions, and respect for the individual's privacy and dignity. When trust is established, individuals are more likely to engage in therapeutic activities and take steps toward their recovery.

- **Peer Support:** Many trauma survivors find comfort and strength in sharing their experiences with others who have had similar experiences. Peer support programs within prisons can provide a sense of community and mutual understanding, which can be incredibly healing for those who feel isolated or misunderstood.

- **Collaboration and Mutuality:** Trauma-informed care emphasizes the importance of collaboration between the individual and their caregivers. In a prison setting, this means involving incarcerated individuals in decisions about their care and encouraging them to take an active role in their healing process. This collaborative approach fosters a sense of agency and empowerment.

- **Empowerment, Voice, and Choice:** Empowering individuals to have a voice in their treatment and recovery is a cornerstone of trauma-informed care. Incarcerated individuals often feel powerless, but by giving them choices and involving them in their own care, they can begin to regain a sense of control over their lives.

- **Cultural Sensitivity:** Trauma-informed care recognizes the importance of cultural, historical, and gender issues in the healing process. It is essential to understand and respect the cultural backgrounds and personal experiences of incarcerated individuals, as these factors play a significant role in how they process trauma and engage in recovery.

Incorporating trauma-informed care into the prison system requires a shift in perspective from one of punishment to one of healing. This can be challenging in environments traditionally focused on control and discipline, but it is necessary for meaningful rehabilitation. Training staff to recognize and respond to signs of trauma, integrating trauma-informed practices into existing programs, and creating new programs specifically designed to address trauma are all critical steps in this process.

A notable example of trauma-informed care in practice is the Connecticut Department of Correction's initiative to train its staff on trauma-informed care principles. This training has helped correctional officers and mental health professionals better understand the behaviors of incarcerated individuals and respond in ways that de-escalate situations and support healing rather than exacerbate trauma. Programs like these are crucial in changing the culture within prisons and ensuring that incarcerated individuals receive the care they need to heal and reintegrate into society successfully.

Mental health services for incarcerated individuals and their families are crucial in addressing the deep and often overlooked impact that incarceration has on mental health. Incarceration not only affects the mental well-being of those behind bars but also has significant repercussions for their families, particularly children. Providing comprehensive mental health services that extend beyond the prison walls can help mitigate these effects, promote healing, and support the reintegration process.

The Mental Health Needs of Incarcerated Individuals

Incarcerated individuals often enter the prison system with existing mental health issues, which can be exacerbated by the harsh realities of prison life. The stress of confinement, separation from loved ones, and the often violent and dehumanizing conditions within prisons can contribute to or worsen mental health conditions such as depression, anxiety, PTSD, and substance use disorders. Despite the high prevalence of these issues, many prisons lack adequate mental health services to address them.

To effectively support incarcerated individuals, mental health services must be comprehensive and accessible. This includes screening and assessment upon entry to identify those in need of immediate mental health care, ongoing therapeutic support, and crisis intervention services. Group therapy, individual counseling, and specialized programs for substance abuse and trauma are essential components of a robust mental health care system within prisons. Additionally, psychiatric services should be available to provide medication management for those with severe mental health conditions.

The mental health of incarcerated individuals is closely linked to the well-being of their families. When a family member is incarcerated, the entire family experiences significant emotional and psychological stress. Children, in particular, are vulnerable to the negative effects of parental incarceration, which can include feelings of abandonment, anxiety, depression, and behavioral problems. The stigma associated with having an incarcerated parent can further compound these issues, leading to social isolation and difficulties in school.

For partners and spouses of incarcerated individuals, the experience can be equally challenging. They may face financial hardship, social stigma, and the emotional burden of maintaining a relationship across the barriers of incarceration. The mental health toll on these family members is often overlooked, yet it is a critical aspect of the broader impact of incarceration.

To address the needs of families affected by incarceration, mental health services must be made available not only to those behind bars but also to their loved ones. Community-based organizations and correctional facilities can work together to offer counseling, support groups, and educational programs for the families of incarcerated individuals. These services can provide a safe space for family members to express their feelings, learn coping strategies, and connect with others who are experiencing similar challenges.

Family therapy can be particularly beneficial, helping to strengthen family bonds, address underlying issues, and prepare for the eventual reintegration of the incarcerated individual into the family unit. Programs that facilitate communication between incarcerated individuals and their families, such as family visitation days, video calls, and letter-writing campaigns, can also play a vital role in maintaining and nurturing these relationships.

For mental health services to be truly effective, they must be part of a continuum of care that begins during incarceration and continues after release. This means that mental health care should not end at the prison gates but should extend into the community to support individuals as they reintegrate into society. Reentry programs that include mental health services can help individuals transition back into their families and communities, reducing the risk of recidivism and promoting long-term stability.

Collaboration between correctional facilities, mental health providers, and community organizations is essential in creating a seamless support system for both incarcerated individuals and their families. This holistic approach recognizes that the mental health of the incarcerated and their loved ones is interconnected and that addressing these needs comprehensively can lead to better outcomes for all involved.

Strategies for Addressing the Intergenerational Impact of Trauma

The intergenerational impact of trauma is a profound issue that can perpetuate cycles of dysfunction, mental health challenges, and criminal behavior across generations. When trauma is not addressed, its effects can ripple through families, affecting not only the individuals who directly experienced it but also their children and grandchildren. In the context of incarcerated fathers, the trauma they endure often leaves lasting imprints on their families, particularly their children, who may struggle with emotional, psychological, and social challenges as a result. Implementing strategies to address and mitigate the intergenerational impact of trauma is crucial for breaking these cycles and fostering resilience and healing within families.

1. Early Intervention and Support for Children

One of the most effective strategies for addressing the intergenerational impact of trauma is to provide early intervention and support for the children of incarcerated fathers. These children are at a higher risk of developing mental health issues, experiencing behavioral problems, and engaging in criminal behavior themselves. Programs that offer counseling, mentoring, and educational support can help these children develop coping skills, build resilience, and process the complex emotions associated with having an incarcerated parent.

Schools, community organizations, and mental health professionals play a key role in identifying at-risk children and connecting them with the resources they need. Initiatives such as after-school programs, trauma-informed educational practices, and family therapy can provide a safe and supportive environment for children to express their feelings and work through their challenges.

2. Family-Centered Approaches

Addressing the intergenerational impact of trauma requires a holistic, family-centered approach that considers the needs of both the incarcerated individual and their family members. Family therapy and counseling programs can help families understand and heal from the trauma they have experienced. These programs should focus on improving communication, strengthening family bonds, and developing strategies for managing stress and emotional difficulties.

Encouraging and facilitating regular communication between incarcerated fathers and their families is also crucial. Maintaining strong family connections can help mitigate the negative effects of incarceration on children and promote a sense of continuity and stability. Programs that allow for in-person visits, video calls, and letter-writing can help preserve these important relationships.

3. Trauma-Informed Parenting Programs

For incarcerated fathers, trauma-informed parenting programs can be an invaluable resource in breaking the cycle of trauma. These programs educate fathers about the effects of trauma on themselves and their children and teach them how to parent in a way that is sensitive to the emotional and psychological needs of their children. By learning how to recognize and respond to signs of trauma, fathers can play a more active role in supporting their children's well-being, even from behind bars.

Programs that offer parenting classes, support groups, and resources on child development can help incarcerated fathers develop the skills and confidence they need to be positive influences in their children's lives. These programs can also provide fathers with tools to manage their own trauma, which is essential for breaking the cycle and preventing the transmission of trauma to the next generation.

4. Community Engagement and Support

Communities have a vital role to play in addressing the intergenerational impact of trauma. Community-based organizations can offer support services for families affected by incarceration, including counseling, financial assistance, and access to social services. These organizations can also advocate for policies that support trauma-informed practices within the criminal justice system and promote the well-being of children and families.

Engaging the broader community in efforts to address the intergenerational impact of trauma can help reduce stigma, raise awareness, and build a network of support for affected families. Community-driven initiatives, such as mentorship programs, family support groups, and public education campaigns, can create a more compassionate and supportive environment for those impacted by incarceration and trauma.

5. Policy and Systemic Changes

Finally, addressing the intergenerational impact of trauma requires systemic changes at the policy level. This includes advocating for criminal justice reforms that prioritize rehabilitation and reintegration over punishment, as well as policies that support family preservation and reunification. Ensuring that mental health services and trauma-informed care are integral parts of the correctional system is essential for breaking the cycle of trauma.

Policies that promote access to mental health care, educational opportunities, and economic support for families affected by incarceration can help reduce the long-term impact of trauma and create a more equitable and just society. Additionally, efforts to reduce mass incarceration and provide alternatives to imprisonment, such as diversion programs and restorative justice practices, can help prevent the intergenerational transmission of trauma in the first place.

The intergenerational impact of trauma is a complex and pervasive issue that requires a multifaceted approach to address effectively. By focusing on early intervention, family-centered care, trauma-informed parenting, community engagement, and systemic change, we can begin to break the cycles of trauma that affect so many families and create a foundation for healing and resilience. These strategies not only support the well-being of individual families but also contribute to the broader goal of creating a more just and compassionate society.

Chapter 16:
Restorative Justice in Florida

Restorative justice (RJ) plays a vital role in healing communities, particularly in states like Florida, where the criminal justice system has long been focused on punishment rather than rehabilitation. Restorative justice shifts the focus from simply penalizing offenders to addressing the harm caused by crime, promoting healing for victims, offenders, and the community. In Florida, where the prison system is vast and the incarcerated population significant, restorative justice offers an alternative framework that can help transform the cycle of crime and retribution into one of healing and reconciliation.

At its core, restorative justice is an approach that seeks to repair the harm caused by criminal behavior. Instead of focusing solely on punishing the offender, it emphasizes accountability, making amends, and addressing the needs of victims and the broader community. Restorative justice provides a platform for offenders to understand the impact of their actions, take responsibility, and work toward repairing the damage they have caused. For victims, it offers a voice in the process, the possibility of closure, and a path to healing.

Florida has started exploring the potential of restorative justice through various pilot programs and community-led initiatives. These programs aim to address the deep-seated issues that arise from crime, including broken relationships and the long-term harm to both individuals and communities. By incorporating restorative justice practices, Florida is taking steps toward reducing recidivism and promoting healing.

In Florida, the integration of restorative justice is still emerging but gaining traction in certain areas. Several counties have begun implementing restorative justice initiatives in both juvenile and adult correctional systems, recognizing the benefits of these practices in reducing reoffending rates and promoting community cohesion. Florida's Office of the State Courts Administrator has noted that restorative justice, particularly in the context of juvenile justice, can significantly reduce recidivism while also addressing the root causes of criminal behavior.

For example, in Sarasota County, a restorative justice program for juveniles focuses on bringing together victims, offenders, and community members to resolve conflicts and address the harm caused by criminal actions. This program has seen success by reducing the reliance on traditional punitive measures like incarceration, which often perpetuate cycles of criminal behavior and isolation from the community. Instead, restorative practices foster personal accountability and encourage offenders to engage with those they have harmed.

The role of restorative justice in healing communities is profound because it promotes understanding, empathy, and reconciliation. When communities adopt restorative justice, they move away from the "us versus them" mentality that often accompanies crime and punishment. Instead, they recognize that both offenders and victims are part of the same social fabric, and their healing is interconnected.

In Florida, where certain communities are disproportionately affected by crime and incarceration—especially low-income communities and communities of color—restorative justice offers a way to rebuild trust and create a shared path toward healing. Programs that facilitate dialogue between offenders and their victims can reduce feelings of isolation and anger while helping communities come together to prevent future harm.

Restorative justice also provides a means for offenders to reintegrate into society more effectively. By emphasizing personal accountability and the importance of making amends, it helps incarcerated individuals develop a sense of purpose and commitment to change. This, in turn, helps heal the relationships they may have damaged within their families and communities. It also addresses one of the key issues that incarcerated fathers in Florida face—the challenge of reconciling with their families and restoring their roles as positive influences in their children's lives.

Restorative justice practices in Florida have shown promising results, particularly in terms of reducing recidivism. Traditional punitive approaches often result in individuals re-entering the criminal justice system after release, perpetuating cycles of crime and imprisonment. However, restorative justice initiatives that focus on rehabilitation, reconciliation, and community healing have been shown to reduce the likelihood of reoffending by addressing the underlying causes of criminal behavior.

Research on restorative justice programs has consistently demonstrated that they lead to lower recidivism rates, particularly when compared to conventional punitive measures. In a study conducted by the University of Florida, restorative justice practices were shown to reduce reoffending rates among juveniles in the state, with many young offenders demonstrating improved emotional and social development after participating in restorative processes. By focusing on healing, both for the offender and the victim, these programs not only reduce crime rates but also strengthen community bonds.

Despite the positive impact of restorative justice, challenges remain in expanding its reach throughout Florida. The state's prison system, like many others, is deeply entrenched in a punitive model that prioritizes incarceration over rehabilitation. Shifting to a restorative framework requires a cultural change within the criminal justice system and broader community awareness of the benefits of restorative practices.

However, there is growing support for restorative justice from advocacy groups, policymakers, and communities across the state. The Florida Restorative Justice Association (FRJA) is actively working to promote restorative practices, offering training and resources to schools, communities, and judicial systems. This work is essential in creating a network of restorative justice programs that can address the needs of both victims and offenders while promoting healing and reconciliation at the community level.

Building on the role of restorative justice in healing communities, a crucial component of this approach is building bridges between victims and offenders. The process of bringing these two parties together in a controlled, respectful, and constructive environment can foster mutual understanding, accountability, and emotional healing. In Florida, where the prison population remains high and many communities are deeply affected by crime, initiatives that focus on victim-offender reconciliation offer a transformative way to address harm while mending the social fabric torn by criminal behavior.

One of the key principles of restorative justice is the belief that dialogue between victims and offenders can promote healing for both parties. For victims, this process can provide an opportunity to express how the crime affected them, receive acknowledgment from the offender, and, in some cases, find closure. For offenders, hearing directly from their victims can be a powerful experience that deepens their understanding of the consequences of their actions. This can lead to greater accountability, remorse, and a genuine desire to make amends.

In Florida, victim-offender dialogue has been incorporated into various restorative justice programs, particularly in juvenile justice settings. Programs such as Victim-Offender Reconciliation

Programs (VORP) aim to humanize both the victim and the offender, moving beyond the traditional adversarial roles often seen in criminal proceedings. These dialogues are typically mediated by trained facilitators who ensure that both parties feel safe, respected, and heard throughout the process.

Building bridges between victims and offenders through restorative justice is not only about dialogue; it's about rebuilding trust and fostering accountability. In many cases, crime causes a breakdown of trust—not just between the victim and the offender but also within the broader community. Restorative justice seeks to repair this by encouraging offenders to take responsibility for their actions and by giving victims a direct role in shaping how restitution or reparation can occur.

In Florida, programs like the Restorative Justice Project at the University of Florida Law School aim to cultivate this sense of accountability. They provide opportunities for offenders to participate in restorative processes that include not only direct conversations with victims but also involvement in community service or other reparative acts that directly address the harm caused. By creating a space for meaningful accountability, these initiatives offer a path to both personal and community healing.

One effective method of building bridges between victims and offenders is through facilitated mediation. Trained mediators guide the conversation to ensure that it remains constructive and focused on healing. In Florida, the use of victim-offender mediation has expanded through initiatives aimed at reducing recidivism and fostering rehabilitation. The Florida Restorative Justice Association (FRJA) is one organization working to bring victim-offender mediation to more communities across the state.

Through this process, victims can express their pain and ask questions that are often left unanswered in traditional court settings. Offenders, in turn, have the chance to explain their actions, offer apologies, and seek ways to make restitution. Studies on restorative justice have shown that when offenders genuinely engage with their victims in this way, they are more likely to understand the full impact of their actions and less likely to re-offend.

Restorative justice programs that focus on building bridges between victims and offenders also address the emotional and psychological wounds caused by crime. Crime often leaves deep scars, not just for the victim but for the offender and the community at large. For victims, the experience of crime can lead to feelings of anger, fear, and helplessness. For offenders, particularly those who are incarcerated, the shame and guilt associated with their actions can become overwhelming, often leading to further alienation and isolation.

By facilitating dialogue and creating opportunities for both parties to express their emotions, restorative justice helps to address these psychological wounds. Programs that focus on emotional healing are especially important in Florida, where incarcerated individuals often come from marginalized communities that have experienced generational trauma. Addressing these emotional wounds in a restorative setting allows for both victims and offenders to move forward in a healthier, more constructive way.

While building bridges between victims and offenders through restorative justice is promising, challenges remain. For many, the idea of directly engaging with the person who harmed them can be daunting, and it requires careful preparation and support. Florida's judicial system, historically focused on punitive measures, is gradually shifting toward more rehabilitative practices, but there is still work to be done in expanding these programs statewide.

However, there are significant opportunities for growth. Programs that focus on mediation and dialogue are gaining traction in Florida, particularly within the juvenile justice system. These programs emphasize the importance of communication and healing over punishment, offering a more effective path to rehabilitation and reintegration. By continuing to invest in restorative justice initiatives, Florida can strengthen its efforts to build bridges between victims and offenders, promoting long-term healing and reducing recidivism across the state.

When it comes to building bridges between victims and offenders, creating opportunities for dialogue and forgiveness is a central tenet of restorative justice. The dialogue between these two parties is crucial not only for fostering understanding but also for facilitating emotional healing and offering a path toward forgiveness. In Florida, where restorative justice programs are gaining recognition, providing structured and safe spaces for this dialogue can be instrumental in breaking cycles of crime, resentment, and hurt.

Opportunities for dialogue between victims and offenders must be carefully constructed to ensure both parties feel supported, respected, and safe. In Florida, organizations and institutions are working to create such spaces through restorative justice programs, where the process is facilitated by trained professionals. These mediators guide the conversation, ensuring that the victim can express their emotions and ask the offender questions that are often left unanswered in the conventional justice process.

One example of a structured program in Florida is the Restorative Justice Circles, used in some counties, where victims, offenders, and community representatives come together in a safe environment to share their stories. The circle format provides a structured yet intimate space where participants can speak candidly and reflect on their experiences. For victims, it can be a crucial moment of being heard, while for offenders, the process helps foster accountability and empathy by allowing them to witness the harm they've caused firsthand.

While not all victims may seek or find forgiveness, restorative justice provides a framework in which forgiveness can naturally emerge through dialogue. The act of expressing remorse and acknowledging the harm caused by one's actions is often a catalyst for forgiveness in these settings. Forgiveness, however, is not forced; rather, it is offered as a potential outcome of the restorative process.

In Florida, restorative justice programs like the Victim Offender Dialogue Program, used particularly in juvenile justice systems, create opportunities for forgiveness by emphasizing mutual understanding and emotional closure. Victims are provided the opportunity to voice their pain and trauma directly to the offender, while offenders are encouraged to take responsibility and demonstrate remorse. This face-to-face interaction can be a profound experience for both parties, allowing them to move beyond the crime toward reconciliation.

Florida's diverse communities present unique challenges and opportunities when it comes to restorative justice. In many communities, particularly those that have experienced generational trauma or high rates of incarceration, the conventional justice system has often exacerbated feelings of alienation and mistrust. By fostering dialogue through restorative justice, these communities have the chance to rebuild trust and cohesion.

Restorative justice programs in Florida are increasingly looking at ways to integrate cultural sensitivity into the dialogue process. Programs that work within communities of color, indigenous populations, and immigrant communities aim to ensure that dialogue reflects the cultural and social contexts of those involved. This culturally attuned approach is essential in creating meaningful opportunities for dialogue, as it acknowledges the unique experiences of Florida's diverse populations and fosters a deeper connection between victims and offenders.

The act of forgiveness, facilitated through dialogue, can be transformative for both victims and offenders, contributing significantly to psychological healing. For victims, forgiving the offender can help reduce feelings of anger, bitterness, and resentment, which often linger long after the crime has occurred. This forgiveness can be a form of emotional liberation, allowing victims to move forward in their lives without the emotional weight of the crime.

For offenders, receiving forgiveness can be equally powerful. It provides a sense of closure and can reinforce their commitment to rehabilitation and change. Forgiveness allows offenders to see themselves as more than just their crimes, encouraging them to take responsibility for their actions while also fostering personal growth and self-worth. In Florida, initiatives like the Juvenile Restorative Justice Program have shown that opportunities for forgiveness, through dialogue, can significantly lower recidivism rates by providing offenders with emotional healing and a stronger sense of accountability.

Despite the clear benefits, creating opportunities for dialogue and forgiveness is not without challenges. Many victims may feel reluctant or emotionally unprepared to confront the person who harmed them. Others may view forgiveness as unnecessary or feel that the crime is unforgivable. In such cases, the role of facilitators becomes crucial in ensuring that the dialogue is voluntary, supportive, and focused on healing rather than forcing an outcome.

In Florida, the development of restorative justice programs often faces systemic challenges, such as the lack of widespread infrastructure or trained personnel to facilitate these dialogues across all communities. However, growing support from local organizations and advocates is helping to expand access to restorative practices that allow for dialogue and forgiveness to become more common outcomes of the justice process.

Creating opportunities for dialogue and forgiveness naturally leads to a deeper exploration of the importance of victim-offender mediation. As seen in the previous section, dialogue is a powerful tool in restorative justice, allowing victims and offenders to communicate openly about the harm caused. Victim-offender mediation formalizes this process, providing a structured, professional setting where both parties can engage in meaningful conversation. This process has proven to be essential in promoting healing, accountability, and even forgiveness, particularly in Florida, where restorative justice initiatives continue to evolve.

The Role of Mediation in Restorative Justice

Victim-offender mediation is a key component of restorative justice, offering a space where both parties can meet under the guidance of a neutral third-party mediator. The mediator facilitates the conversation, ensuring that it remains respectful and productive, while also helping both the victim and the offender articulate their feelings, experiences, and expectations. This structured approach offers a balance of emotional support and practical negotiation, where the offender is encouraged to take responsibility for their actions and the victim can participate in determining how the harm can be repaired.

In Florida, programs like the Victim Offender Dialogue Program have implemented mediation strategies to address both juvenile and adult cases, helping to reduce reoffending and enhance victim satisfaction with the justice process. These programs highlight the importance of creating an environment where both parties feel safe and empowered to engage in an honest and transformative conversation. Studies on these programs in Florida and elsewhere show that participants in victim-offender mediation often report a stronger sense of closure and emotional healing compared to those who go through the traditional justice system.

Mediation serves as a crucial bridge for victims and offenders to move from mere dialogue to actionable outcomes. In traditional criminal justice, offenders are often punished without fully understanding the personal impact of their actions, while victims rarely have a say in the legal proceedings. Mediation shifts this dynamic, placing both parties at the center of the process. The offender's acknowledgment of their wrongdoing, combined with the victim's input on how to repair the harm, leads to a more personalized and meaningful resolution.

In Florida, victim-offender mediation has been particularly effective in juvenile justice cases, where the emphasis is on rehabilitation rather than punishment. Through mediation, young offenders are given the opportunity to take responsibility for their actions in a way that fosters personal growth and accountability, while victims are able to see justice served in a way that directly addresses their needs. This process is vital in helping both parties heal and reestablish a sense of safety and trust within their community.

Victim-offender mediation also provides significant emotional benefits for both parties. Victims are given a platform to express their emotions, share their stories, and ask questions that often go unanswered in a courtroom. They can also negotiate a restorative resolution that meets their personal needs, whether that involves a formal apology, community service, or reparations. For offenders, the process of facing their victim and hearing firsthand how their actions caused harm can lead to profound emotional and psychological shifts. This deeper understanding often results in genuine remorse and a desire to make amends.

Florida's restorative justice programs highlight how mediation can foster these emotional outcomes. In fact, data from restorative programs indicate that both victims and offenders report higher levels of satisfaction with the justice process when mediation is involved, compared to more traditional punitive approaches.

Mediation allows for a deeper emotional connection that can be transformative, reducing the likelihood of reoffending while also promoting long-term healing.

One of the key reasons mediations is so effective is due to the presence of trained facilitators who guide the process. These professionals help ensure that both parties feel comfortable and that the dialogue remains focused on healing and resolution. In Florida, the expansion of victim-offender mediation programs has involved training more facilitators to handle complex cases, particularly those involving violence or significant emotional trauma. Trained facilitators are essential for navigating these difficult conversations, helping to keep the discussion balanced and productive.

By prioritizing victim-offender mediation as a key aspect of restorative justice, Florida can continue to shift the focus from punishment to healing. This process not only aids in the emotional recovery of victims but also fosters a greater sense of responsibility and personal growth in offenders, ultimately contributing to healthier, safer communities across the state.

Chapter 17:
From Awareness to Action

In the transition from awareness to action, one of the most crucial steps is motivating individuals and communities to actively engage in efforts for social change. While raising awareness is vital, meaningful progress only occurs when people are driven to contribute to the cause. In Florida and beyond, the importance of this step cannot be overstated, particularly in addressing issues like prison reform, restorative justice, and community rehabilitation. Engaging individuals and communities require both education and empowerment, ensuring that people not only understand the issues but also feel equipped and motivated to take action.

The Power of Personal Stories and Lived Experience

One of the most effective ways to motivate individuals and communities is by sharing personal stories and lived experiences. In the context of restorative justice and prison reform, hearing directly from those who have been impacted—such as incarcerated fathers, victims of crime, or family members—can inspire others to get involved. Personal stories humanize abstract issues, creating an emotional connection that drives people to take action.

In Florida, several advocacy organizations have harnessed the power of personal storytelling to encourage community involvement. Groups like the Florida Restorative Justice Association (FRJA) regularly feature stories from individuals who have gone through restorative justice programs, providing a platform for those voices that might otherwise go unheard. These stories often serve as a call to action, motivating listeners to advocate for reform and get involved in local efforts to support restorative justice initiatives.

Education is another key element in motivating communities to take action. Many individuals are unaware of the systemic issues surrounding mass incarceration, the prison-industrial complex, or the barriers to rehabilitation for incarcerated individuals. Therefore, informing communities about these topics is a necessary first step. Educational campaigns, public forums, and workshops can help demystify complex issues, making them more accessible to the general public.

In Florida, organizations working on prison reform and restorative justice regularly host events and seminars aimed at educating the public. By providing clear, factual information about the state's criminal justice system, these initiatives help mobilize communities, encouraging them to advocate for policy changes. For example, the Florida Justice Institute (FJI) has developed educational resources and outreach programs to inform the public about prison conditions, the challenges faced by incarcerated individuals, and the need for reform. Once individuals and communities are educated about these issues, they are more likely to become advocates for change.

Community-based approaches are crucial when motivating individuals to become involved. Localized efforts, such as town halls, neighborhood meetings, and community outreach, are often more effective in encouraging participation than large, statewide campaigns. When people see that the issues directly affect their community, they are more likely to feel a sense of responsibility to take action.

In Florida, grassroots organizations working in the field of prison reform often emphasize localized engagement. These organizations focus on building relationships with community leaders, churches, schools, and local activists to foster a sense of collective responsibility for addressing issues such as prison overcrowding, lack of mental health resources, and the failure to rehabilitate incarcerated individuals. For example, local chapters of the Southern Poverty Law Center (SPLC) engage communities in conversations about the role of the prison system and the need for restorative justice, encouraging direct involvement in advocacy efforts.

Finally, motivating individuals requires empowering them with the tools and knowledge necessary to take action. People are more likely to get involved when they believe their efforts will make a tangible difference. Therefore, providing clear, actionable steps— such as contacting legislators, attending local meetings, or joining advocacy groups—helps translate awareness into active participation.

In Florida, groups advocating for prison reform and restorative justice have developed various ways to empower individuals. For instance, the Florida Campaign for Criminal Justice Reform (FCCJR) provides its supporters with tools such as letter-writing campaigns, petitions, and advocacy toolkits to make engagement as accessible as possible. By giving people actionable steps, these organizations ensure that individuals feel capable of making a meaningful contribution to the movement.

The next critical step is building coalitions and partnerships for change. While individual efforts are essential, large-scale transformation in areas such as prison reform and restorative justice requires collaboration between multiple stakeholders. Effective coalitions and partnerships bring together diverse voices— advocates, policymakers, community leaders, and affected individuals—to pool resources, share knowledge, and amplify the impact of their collective efforts. In Florida, as elsewhere, building these alliances is crucial to pushing for systemic change.

When individuals and organizations unite under a shared cause, their combined efforts can achieve much more than any one group could on its own. Coalitions are particularly effective because they allow different groups to bring unique strengths and perspectives to the table. In the case of criminal justice reform in Florida, coalitions of community organizations, legal experts, and activists have proven instrumental in pushing for legislative changes, increasing public awareness, and holding institutions accountable.

For example, the Florida Rights Restoration Coalition (FRRC) played a pivotal role in the passage of Amendment 4, which restored voting rights to over a million formerly incarcerated individuals. The FRRC brought together various civil rights groups, faith-based organizations, and community leaders to advocate for this change, creating a powerful movement that had a statewide and national impact. This coalition leveraged the strength of its diverse partners to push for a common goal, demonstrating the effectiveness of collaborative action.

Building effective coalitions and partnerships starts with establishing shared goals and clear objectives. For change to be sustainable, all parties involved must agree on a common vision, such as reducing recidivism, improving mental health services for incarcerated individuals, or expanding restorative justice programs. Once these goals are defined, coalition members can determine how to allocate resources—whether it's funding, manpower, or expertise—to maximize their impact.

In Florida, partnerships between advocacy organizations like the Southern Poverty Law Center (SPLC) and the Florida Justice Institute (FJI) have created a network of support for incarcerated individuals, working together to fight for improved prison conditions and reform policies that address systemic inequities. These partnerships allow each organization to focus on its specific areas of expertise, whether it's legal advocacy, public education, or direct services, while working in unison toward larger, systemic change.

A successful coalition also requires the engagement of key stakeholders, including policymakers, law enforcement, and even private sector organizations. In Florida, some advocacy coalitions have partnered with local legislators to push forward criminal justice reform bills, ensuring that the voices of those impacted by the prison system are heard in state government. Engaging with policymakers can help turn grassroots activism into tangible legislative outcomes, bridging the gap between community efforts and formal, institutional change.

At the same time, engaging law enforcement agencies in these coalitions can be valuable in developing comprehensive strategies for prison reform. In some cases, law enforcement officers are in a unique position to offer insights into the criminal justice system's inner workings and can be partners in pushing for change that aligns with public safety and rehabilitation goals.

One effective model for coalition-building in Florida has been seen in initiatives aimed at reducing youth incarceration rates. The Florida Juvenile Justice Association (FJJA) has partnered with various stakeholders, including community organizations, legal professionals, and government agencies, to advocate for restorative practices in juvenile justice. This coalition has helped create alternatives to incarceration for young offenders, such as diversion programs and community-based interventions. By working together, the coalition has been able to push for changes that reduce the state's reliance on incarceration, focusing instead on rehabilitation and support for at-risk youth.

In addition to state-level coalitions, Florida has also seen partnerships that bridge national and local efforts. Organizations like the American Civil Liberties Union (ACLU) and the National Association for the Advancement of Colored People (NAACP) often work alongside Florida-based groups to advocate for prison reform and criminal justice policy changes, leveraging national resources and platforms to support localized efforts.

While building coalitions is a powerful strategy, it's not without challenges. Aligning different groups with varying priorities and methods can be difficult, and maintaining cohesion over time requires ongoing communication and compromise. Additionally, ensuring that marginalized voices—such as those of incarcerated individuals and their families—are given a central role in these coalitions is crucial for truly impactful change.

For coalitions to thrive, there must be an emphasis on inclusivity, ensuring that everyone from community members to policymakers has a seat at the table. In Florida, organizations like the Florida Council for Incarcerated and Formerly Incarcerated Women and Girls work to ensure that the most affected populations are part of the conversation, amplifying voices that are often left out of mainstream advocacy.

Building coalitions and partnerships is essential in amplifying advocacy efforts, creating broad support for reform, and pooling resources toward common goals. From local grassroots initiatives to national alliances, partnerships provide the structural foundation needed to sustain long-term, systemic change.

This naturally leads to the next critical element: developing effective advocacy strategies, where coalitions can leverage their collective power to influence policy, public opinion, and institutional practices. By coordinating efforts, defining shared objectives, and mobilizing resources, coalitions can create a roadmap for achieving meaningful change. Advocacy strategies will be discussed in the next section as we continue exploring the pathways from awareness to action.

Once coalitions are formed, with diverse stakeholders united by a common purpose, the next task is to create clear and actionable advocacy plans to achieve their goals. Effective advocacy strategies are vital in driving systemic change, influencing policymakers, and shifting public perceptions. In Florida, where coalitions have been instrumental in criminal justice reform, developing these strategies requires a multi-faceted approach that leverages the power of grassroots activism, media engagement, and legislative advocacy.

Effective advocacy begins with a clear understanding of the coalition's objectives. Whether the goal is to push for legislative reforms, raise public awareness, or create community-based alternatives to incarceration, advocacy strategies must be tailored to address the specific goals of the coalition. For example, if the goal is to reduce recidivism rates among incarcerated fathers in Florida, the coalition might focus on expanding access to mental health services, rehabilitation programs, and family support networks within the prison system.

One successful advocacy approach used by Florida-based coalitions is combining public education campaigns with legislative advocacy. The Florida Campaign for Criminal Justice Reform (FCCJR), for instance, has advocated for sentencing reforms, improved prison conditions, and alternatives to incarceration. By engaging the public through education and rallying support for specific legislative initiatives, FCCJR has made progress in influencing criminal justice policies at both state and local levels. Tailoring advocacy strategies to specific legislative goals has allowed the coalition to target its efforts where it can have the most immediate impact.

Grassroots mobilization is a core component of many effective advocacy strategies, particularly in Florida, where community-based efforts have played a pivotal role in reform movements. Mobilizing community members to participate in advocacy efforts not only builds public support but also creates pressure on policymakers to take action. Grassroots advocacy often includes organizing rallies, town hall meetings, and signature petitions, as well as encouraging direct communication with elected officials.

In Florida, grassroots efforts led by organizations such as the Dream Defenders have been successful in mobilizing communities to push for criminal justice reform. The Dream Defenders, founded in response to the killing of Trayvon Martin, have used grassroots organizing to advocate for the end of the school-to-prison pipeline and to demand accountability in the criminal justice system. By engaging directly with affected communities, they have built a broad base of support for reform initiatives, demonstrating how grassroots advocacy can drive systemic change.

A critical component of any advocacy strategy is engaging with lawmakers and other key decision-makers. Legislative advocacy, including lobbying efforts, is essential for translating the coalition's goals into policy change. In Florida, criminal justice reform coalitions often collaborate with advocacy groups, legal organizations, and political allies to draft, promote, and support legislation that aligns with their objectives.

For example, the Florida Justice Institute (FJI), a legal advocacy organization, has partnered with coalitions working to reform the state's prison system. By engaging in direct lobbying efforts, FJI has worked to push forward legislation aimed at improving prison conditions, increasing access to rehabilitation programs, and addressing racial disparities in sentencing. Legislative advocacy requires coalitions to build relationships with lawmakers, provide research and evidence to support policy proposals, and consistently advocate for reforms that align with their goals.

Engaging the Media and Shaping Public Opinion

Effective advocacy also involves engaging with the media to shape public opinion and raise awareness of critical issues. Coalitions can leverage media platforms to amplify their message, highlight the stories of those directly impacted by the criminal justice system, and build broader support for their cause. This is particularly important in Florida, where public opinion has historically influenced the outcome of criminal justice reform efforts.

Media engagement strategies include publishing op-eds, holding press conferences, and using social media to spread awareness. For example, during the campaign for Amendment 4 in Florida, which aimed to restore voting rights to formerly incarcerated individuals, advocates strategically used media platforms to humanize the issue. By sharing the stories of those directly affected and framing the issue as one of fairness and redemption, they were able to shift public opinion in favor of the amendment. Media engagement helped build momentum for the successful passage of the initiative.

Social media also plays a vital role in modern advocacy strategies. Platforms like Twitter, Facebook, and Instagram provide advocates with the ability to reach large audiences quickly, engage directly with supporters, and respond to real-time developments. In Florida, coalitions have effectively used social media campaigns to raise awareness, mobilize supporters, and apply pressure on lawmakers to enact reforms.

Data and Research-Driven Advocacy

Another important element in developing effective advocacy strategies is using data and research to support the coalition's goals. Advocacy efforts are more persuasive when backed by factual information, whether it's about prison conditions, recidivism rates, or the financial costs of incarceration. Research-driven advocacy provides coalitions with the evidence they need to make compelling arguments for reform and demonstrate the long-term benefits of their proposed changes.

For example, the Southern Poverty Law Center (SPLC) has used data on the racial disparities in Florida's prison system to advocate for sentencing reforms and alternatives to incarceration. By presenting research that highlights how current policies disproportionately affect communities of color, the SPLC has been able to build a stronger case for reform. Data-driven advocacy helps coalition members build credibility, engage with policymakers on a deeper level, and appeal to a wider audience.

In conclusion, developing effective advocacy strategies is essential for turning coalition goals into actionable change. By tailoring strategies to specific objectives, mobilizing grassroots support, engaging lawmakers and the media, and using research to strengthen their case, coalitions can maximize their impact. From grassroots mobilization to legislative advocacy, these strategies empower coalitions in Florida to push for meaningful reforms in the criminal justice system.

The next step in this journey is to create a clear roadmap for grassroots activism, where community members are equipped with the tools and resources to continue advocating for change at the local level. This will be explored in the following section as we delve into how to translate advocacy into sustained, community-driven action.

Creating a roadmap for grassroots activism is a vital step in translating awareness into sustained, community-driven efforts for change. Grassroots activism focuses on mobilizing ordinary people to take action on critical social, political, or economic issues. In the context of Florida's criminal justice reform, a well-defined roadmap helps individuals and communities understand how they can contribute to advocacy efforts, creating a bottom-up approach to influence policy and systemic change.

The first step in creating a roadmap for grassroots activism is defining the mission and setting clear, attainable goals. These goals should reflect the broader objectives of the coalition or advocacy group but break them down into actionable steps for community members. For instance, in Florida, if the goal is to reduce recidivism among incarcerated fathers, grassroots efforts may focus on advocating for expanded rehabilitation programs, improving prison conditions, or increasing access to mental health services.

Clear goals allow activists to remain focused and ensure that all efforts are working towards a common objective. Additionally, setting milestones—such as influencing specific legislation or garnering a certain level of community participation—helps measure progress and maintain momentum.

Grassroots activism is most effective when communities are informed and aware of the issues at hand. In Florida, criminal justice reform movements often start by educating community members about the flaws in the prison system, the need for restorative justice, or the benefits of rehabilitation programs for incarcerated individuals and their families. This can be achieved through workshops, town hall meetings, and informational campaigns.

Providing accessible, digestible information is key. Complex issues like mass incarceration, systemic racism, and mental health care disparities can seem overwhelming, so breaking them down into understandable terms helps foster engagement. Grassroots movements, such as the Dream Defenders in Florida, have been successful in educating communities about the root causes of these issues and encouraging activism by making the information relatable and actionable.

Once people are educated about the issues, the next step is to mobilize them into action. This can involve organizing community events, protests, or signature campaigns that draw attention to specific causes. For example, Florida's Second Chances Campaign, which led to the passage of Amendment 4 (restoring voting rights to formerly incarcerated individuals), relied heavily on grassroots mobilization. Activists engaged with people directly, gathering signatures and educating the public on the importance of the issue.

Mobilizing community members also includes fostering relationships with local organizations, churches, and schools, as these institutions can serve as hubs for activism. Churches and community centers in particular play a crucial role in Florida's grassroots movements, offering space for organizing meetings and serving as trusted sources of information for local residents.

For grassroots activism to be successful, individuals must be equipped with the right tools and resources. This can include training on how to engage with local legislators, guidelines for organizing petitions or protests or providing sample letters and emails that individuals can send to their elected officials. Resources like these make it easier for community members to take action and participate in advocacy efforts without feeling overwhelmed.

In Florida, organizations like the Florida Justice Institute (FJI) and the Southern Poverty Law Center (SPLC) provide legal toolkits, research data, and advocacy guidelines to help grassroots movements. They support activists in understanding their legal rights, crafting policy recommendations, and engaging effectively with lawmakers.

Using Digital Platforms to Amplify the Movement

In today's digital age, online platforms are critical for amplifying grassroots movements. Social media platforms such as Twitter, Facebook, and Instagram can be used to share information, mobilize supporters, and apply pressure on decision-makers. Digital organizing allows activists to reach a wider audience and engage with people beyond their immediate communities.

For instance, during Florida's Amendment 4 campaign, digital platforms played a key role in raising awareness about the importance of restoring voting rights for formerly incarcerated individuals. Activists shared stories, statistics, and calls to action across social media, rallying supporters from across the state and even attracting national attention. Digital organizing tools, including online petitions, email campaigns, and social media advocacy, can help transform grassroots efforts into large-scale movements.

One of the biggest challenges in grassroots activism is maintaining long-term engagement. Once a campaign or a key objective is achieved, it is essential to sustain momentum and continue working toward the next goal. Creating a sustainable roadmap for activism involves building ongoing relationships with community members, hosting regular events, and keeping activists engaged through updates and progress reports.

In Florida, movements like the Florida Rights Restoration Coalition (FRRC) have sustained long-term engagement by focusing on ongoing issues, such as expanding the reach of Amendment 4 and addressing new legislative challenges. They keep their base of supporters informed about upcoming initiatives and opportunities for continued involvement.

Additionally, it's important to train the next generation of activists, empowering young people to take leadership roles within grassroots movements. By mentoring new activists and providing them with the tools to continue the work, coalitions can ensure that the movement remains strong over time.

Finally, a key part of any roadmap for grassroots activism is developing partnerships with other advocacy organizations. Collaborating with national groups such as the ACLU or local entities like the Florida Council for Incarcerated and Formerly Incarcerated Women and Girls allows grassroots movements to leverage broader resources, gain credibility, and scale their efforts. By working together, grassroots movements can create a more unified voice and maximize their impact.

In conclusion, creating a roadmap for grassroots activism involves a multi-step approach: defining clear goals, educating and mobilizing the community, providing tools for advocacy, leveraging digital platforms, sustaining long-term engagement, and developing strategic partnerships. By following this roadmap, grassroots movements in Florida can effectively contribute to criminal justice reform and ensure that their voices are heard on both local and national stages.

Chapter 18:
Cultivating Empathy and Healing

E mpathy-based programs for incarcerated individuals and the community are essential for fostering understanding and reducing recidivism. These programs focus on helping individuals recognize the consequences of their actions and cultivate a sense of responsibility for harm done, while also encouraging the community to see incarcerated individuals as capable of change. Florida has seen an increasing need for these types of initiatives, as many incarcerated fathers, in particular, face challenges related to broken family ties, generational trauma, and societal stigma.

Empathy Programs Inside Prisons

Empathy-based programs within prisons help inmates develop emotional intelligence, social awareness, and accountability. One effective model is restorative justice circles or dialogues, where incarcerated individuals engage in facilitated conversations about their actions, the harm they have caused, and how they can make amends. Such programs encourage participants to confront the emotional and psychological effects of their behavior on others, including victims, families, and communities.

An example of this is the Restorative Justice Project at Florida State Prison, which works with incarcerated men to teach them communication and conflict resolution skills. The program encourages participants to reflect on the impact of their crimes and engage in discussions about how they can repair relationships with their families and society. Inmates often report a deeper understanding of the harm they caused, leading to emotional growth and a commitment to positive change.

Empathy-building programs can also include storytelling workshops or creative writing groups, where incarcerated individuals express their emotions and share their stories in a non-judgmental setting. By sharing their experiences, they learn to articulate feelings of regret, guilt, and hope for redemption. Programs like The Writer's Block, operating in Florida prisons, offer inmates the opportunity to write about their personal experiences, often leading to emotional breakthroughs that foster empathy for themselves and others. These programs help participants not only understand their own emotions but also the feelings and perspectives of those they have harmed.

Empathy-based programs are not just about rehabilitation within prisons; they are also about bridging the gap between incarcerated individuals and the communities they will eventually rejoin. One of the biggest challenges incarcerated individuals face upon release is reintegration into society. By involving the community in empathy-building initiatives, we can reduce the stigma that often follows formerly incarcerated individuals, making it easier for them to reenter society and avoid recidivism.

One approach is to invite community members into prisons to participate in restorative dialogues or mentorship programs. In these settings, community members and incarcerated individuals engage in discussions about crime, punishment, and forgiveness. These exchanges can be transformative, as they humanize incarcerated individuals and help the community see them as more than just their crimes. The Florida Restorative Justice Association has piloted several programs where community volunteers meet with incarcerated men and women to foster open dialogue. The impact is profound, as both parties often leave with a deeper understanding of the human condition and the power of empathy in healing.

Another model for connecting incarcerated individuals with their communities is through victim-offender reconciliation programs (VORPs). These programs provide a structured environment where victims and offenders can meet face-to-face to discuss the crime, its impact, and ways to move forward. Such encounters help incarcerated individuals confront the real consequences of their actions while offering victims the chance to express their pain and, in some cases, find closure. Florida's Victim Offender Dialogue Program has helped facilitate numerous encounters where both victims and offenders have reported healing and greater empathy for one another.

Empathy-based programs for the broader community are equally important in cultivating understanding and reducing the societal stigma that follows incarcerated individuals. Public perception plays a critical role in how formerly incarcerated individuals are treated after release. Without empathy, communities can become hostile and unwelcoming, increasing the chances of reoffending. Therefore, empathy training programs can be offered to community members, focusing on understanding the challenges of reintegration and fostering supportive environments for returning citizens.

Workshops that educate the public on the systemic issues of incarceration, such as racial disparities, mental health challenges, and generational trauma, can foster a more compassionate view of formerly incarcerated individuals. Programs like Empathy in Action, which has been introduced in some Florida schools and community centers, teach people to consider the circumstances that lead individuals into the criminal justice system, helping them understand that many offenders are products of systemic failures rather than inherently bad people.

Through community education and awareness initiatives, empathy-based programs can challenge the fear and bias that often accompany the release of incarcerated individuals. These programs encourage community members to see formerly incarcerated individuals as capable of rehabilitation and reintegration, rather than as permanent threats.

However, when it comes to a paradigm shift from traditional punitive approaches to a more rehabilitative and community-centric model, it is important to Incorporate restorative justice (RJ) practices into the criminal justice system. While the conventional system focuses on punishment and deterrence, restorative justice emphasizes healing for both victims and offenders, fostering accountability, and promoting reconciliation. Restorative justice is not merely a tool for addressing individual cases but a transformative approach that seeks to reframe how society deals with crime and justice.

Restorative justice practices are grounded in the belief that crime is not just a violation of law, but a harm done to people, relationships, and communities. As such, RJ focuses on repairing this harm by encouraging dialogue, mutual understanding, and cooperation among victims, offenders, and the community. Programs can include victim-offender mediation, restorative circles, family group conferencing, and community reparation boards.

In Florida, restorative justice practices are slowly gaining traction. The Florida Restorative Justice Association (FRJA) has been instrumental in promoting RJ frameworks in various communities and correctional settings. Programs like these are designed to create opportunities for offenders to acknowledge the impact of their actions, take responsibility, and make amends in ways that directly benefit the victims and the wider community. This stands in stark contrast to traditional incarceration, which often isolates offenders from society and focuses solely on punishment.

One of the primary benefits of incorporating RJ into the criminal justice system is its potential to reduce recidivism rates. Research has shown that offenders who participate in restorative justice programs are significantly less likely to re-offend compared to those who go through the traditional court system. For example, a study conducted by the Florida Department of Juvenile Justice found that juveniles who completed RJ programs had lower recidivism rates than those who went through traditional court proceedings. By addressing the root causes of criminal behavior, such as unmet emotional needs, trauma, and poor conflict resolution skills, restorative justice fosters long-term behavioral change.

Another advantage of restorative justice is that it offers victims an active role in the justice process. Rather than being sidelined, victims in RJ programs can directly communicate with offenders, express their feelings, and work toward resolution. This process often helps victims find closure and healing, reducing the emotional toll that crime can have. In fact, surveys conducted by the Victim-Offender Dialogue Program in Florida revealed that over 80% of participants felt a sense of resolution and satisfaction after engaging in RJ practices.

Furthermore, RJ can alleviate some of the financial strain on Florida's criminal justice system. Incarceration is expensive, and Florida has one of the largest prison populations in the United States. Implementing restorative justice practices could reduce the burden on the state's correctional facilities by offering alternative resolutions to incarceration. By diverting low-risk offenders to RJ programs, the state can reduce overcrowding in prisons and lower the costs associated with housing, feeding, and supervising inmates. For example, community-based RJ programs often require fewer resources and can be implemented at a fraction of the cost of incarceration.

However, despite its many advantages, incorporating restorative justice into Florida's criminal justice system is not without challenges. One of the primary obstacles is resistance from stakeholders who are accustomed to traditional punitive approaches. Prosecutors, law enforcement, and even some members of the public may view RJ as being too lenient on offenders. There is often a perception that restorative justice does not provide the necessary level of punishment or deterrence, especially for more serious offenses.

To address this concern, advocates of RJ must emphasize the program's dual focus on accountability and rehabilitation. Offenders are not simply forgiven for their actions but are held responsible in a way that requires them to actively repair the harm they have caused. By demonstrating the long-term benefits of RJ—such as reduced recidivism, cost savings, and community healing—advocates can work to shift public and institutional attitudes.

Another challenge is ensuring that restorative justice practices are applied equitably across the criminal justice system. In many cases, RJ programs are offered primarily to juveniles or low-level offenders, while individuals convicted of more serious crimes are excluded. However, restorative justice principles can be effective even in cases involving serious offenses, as long as both victims and offenders are willing to participate. Programs like Florida's Victim Offender Dialogue Program have shown that even in cases of violent crime, RJ can provide a pathway for healing and resolution that the traditional justice system often cannot.

Incorporating restorative justice practices into Florida's criminal justice system requires a coordinated effort among law enforcement agencies, courts, correctional institutions, and community organizations. It involves a shift in mindset from punitive to rehabilitative justice and a commitment to providing resources for RJ programs to thrive. Expanding training for law enforcement and corrections officers on restorative justice principles is a crucial step in this process. Additionally, legislation that supports the implementation and funding of RJ programs in Florida is necessary to ensure widespread adoption. The role of law enforcement and correctional officers is critical in shaping the experiences of individuals within the criminal justice system. However, many of these individuals have histories of trauma that contribute to their criminal behavior, making it essential for officers to approach interactions with a trauma-informed mindset. Training law enforcement and correctional officers in trauma-informed care can significantly improve outcomes for both the incarcerated population and the system itself. By understanding the underlying effects of trauma, officers can foster environments that reduce harm, prevent re-traumatization, and encourage rehabilitation.

Understanding Trauma and Its Impact

Trauma can stem from a variety of experiences, such as abuse, neglect, violence, or systemic injustice. For many incarcerated individuals, trauma is a significant factor in their life trajectory, often contributing to substance abuse, mental health challenges, and criminal behavior. The Substance Abuse and Mental Health Services Administration (SAMHSA) defines trauma as an event or series of events that are physically or emotionally harmful, with lasting adverse effects on an individual's functioning and well-being.

A significant percentage of incarcerated individuals in the U.S. have experienced trauma prior to their incarceration. According to a report by the **Substance Abuse and Mental Health Services Administration (SAMHSA)**, around 75% of individuals in the criminal justice system have a history of trauma, including experiences such as physical abuse, neglect, or exposure to violence.[9] This makes trauma-informed care (TIC) crucial in shaping how law enforcement and correctional officers interact with individuals in custody. Without recognizing trauma's pervasive effects, law enforcement officers may unintentionally escalate situations, leading to further emotional damage for those already vulnerable. TIC emphasizes safety, trust, collaboration, and empowerment, which

---

[9] SAMHSA Trauma and Justice Report:
https://store.samhsa.gov/sites/default/files/d7/priv/sma14-4884.pdf

can dramatically improve how officers engage with the incarcerated population.

Trauma-informed care shifts the focus from "What's wrong with you?" to "What happened to you?" This simple but powerful change in perspective allows law enforcement officers to view behavior as a symptom of past trauma rather than merely defiance or resistance. For example, an individual displaying aggression or refusal to cooperate during an arrest may be reacting to triggers from past trauma, such as violent encounters with authority figures. If an officer is trained in trauma-informed care, they can de-escalate the situation, rather than resorting to force, by addressing the individual's emotional state with empathy and understanding.

In Florida, law enforcement agencies like the Florida Department of Corrections (FDC) have begun to recognize the value of trauma-informed approaches. The FDC has implemented pilot programs to train officers in de-escalation techniques that incorporate trauma awareness. These programs focus on reducing the use of force and improving communication between officers and inmates. In one such program, officers reported that using trauma-informed care helped them avoid violent confrontations and build rapport with the incarcerated population, ultimately leading to safer environments for both officers and inmates.

Correctional officers are on the front lines of managing the day-to-day lives of incarcerated individuals. In many cases, they are responsible for managing individuals who are experiencing severe emotional distress, often rooted in trauma. Without adequate training in trauma-informed care, correctional officers may respond to such distress with punitive measures that only exacerbate the situation. For example, placing an inmate in solitary confinement for disruptive behavior may further isolate and traumatize them, leading to a vicious cycle of misconduct and punishment.

By training correctional officers in TIC, correctional facilities can promote healing rather than harm. Trauma-informed care within correctional settings involves teaching officers to recognize the signs of trauma, such as hypervigilance, emotional numbness, or erratic behavior, and to respond with appropriate support. This could involve using calming techniques, offering mental health resources, or simply providing a safe space for the inmate to express their emotions without fear of retribution. In Florida, the Trauma Recovery and Empowerment Model (TREM) is one such initiative that trains correctional staff to work with trauma survivors, creating a more supportive and less punitive environment within the state's prisons.

The benefits of trauma-informed care training for law enforcement and correctional officers are multifaceted. First, it leads to better outcomes for inmates by reducing re-traumatization, improving mental health, and encouraging positive behavioral changes. By creating a safer, more supportive environment, incarcerated individuals are more likely to engage in rehabilitation programs, address their underlying trauma, and prepare for successful reentry into society.

Second, trauma-informed training reduces the incidence of violence within correctional facilities. When officers approach situations with empathy and an understanding of trauma, they are better equipped to de-escalate conflicts before they turn violent. This not only protects inmates from harm but also ensures the safety of correctional staff. Research from the National Institute of Justice (NIJ) indicates that facilities with trauma-informed practices see fewer instances of use-of-force incidents and disciplinary actions, creating a more stable and manageable environment for all.

Third, TIC training improves officer well-being. Officers working in high-stress environments, such as prisons, are often exposed to secondary trauma, which can lead to burnout, emotional exhaustion, and even post-traumatic stress disorder (PTSD).

Trauma-informed training helps officers recognize the signs of trauma in themselves and their colleagues, providing them with tools to manage stress and avoid burnout.

While the benefits of trauma-informed care are clear, implementing such training on a wide scale face challenges. Limited resources, resistance from officers who are used to traditional punitive approaches, and a lack of comprehensive TIC curricula in law enforcement training programs are all obstacles to adoption. However, as awareness of the importance of trauma-informed care grows, particularly in states like Florida, more agencies are beginning to prioritize this training.

Empathy Training Programs for the General Public

Empathy training programs are not just beneficial within correctional institutions; they also play a critical role in shaping how the general public perceives and interacts with individuals who have been impacted by the criminal justice system. These programs aim to foster a deeper understanding of the circumstances that lead to incarceration, emphasizing the importance of empathy in creating more inclusive communities. By educating the public about trauma, poverty, systemic inequalities, and the challenges faced by formerly incarcerated individuals, empathy training encourages people to replace judgment with understanding.

In Florida, various organizations and community initiatives have started offering workshops and seminars focused on building empathy toward marginalized groups, including incarcerated individuals. One example is the Florida Restorative Justice Association (FRJA), which organizes community-based workshops aimed at fostering understanding between former inmates and the general public. These sessions help bridge the gap between these groups, making reintegration into society smoother for those leaving the correctional system.

Programs such as these often employ interactive exercises, role-playing, and storytelling to humanize the experiences of individuals affected by the criminal justice system. By placing participants in hypothetical scenarios that mimic the challenges faced by formerly incarcerated individuals, empathy training creates a more compassionate mindset. Community members begin to see individuals beyond their criminal records, recognizing the traumas and social contexts that may have contributed to their incarceration. This shift in perspective can lead to community support for reform efforts and even direct involvement in rehabilitation and restorative justice initiatives.

Moreover, empathy training for the general public can help reduce the stigma associated with incarceration. A less stigmatized environment is key to helping former inmates reintegrate into society, access jobs, housing, and other essential services, ultimately reducing recidivism rates. With proper support from the public, individuals transitioning out of the criminal justice system have a better chance of leading successful, productive lives.

Measuring the success of empathy-based initiatives is crucial for ensuring that these programs are not only effective but also adaptable to meet the needs of diverse populations. Evaluating the impact of such programs involves both qualitative and quantitative approaches, assessing how these initiatives affect attitudes, behaviors, and outcomes for both participants and the formerly incarcerated.

In Florida, organizations involved in empathy training and restorative justice programs have developed several metrics to evaluate their success. For example, surveys and pre- and post-program evaluations can be used to measure changes in attitudes among community members who participate in empathy training. These tools assess shifts in empathy levels, willingness to engage with formerly incarcerated individuals, and support for restorative justice policies.

Additionally, some programs track recidivism rates, employment outcomes, and community reintegration success for formerly incarcerated individuals as indirect indicators of empathy-based initiatives. In Florida's Operation New Hope, a program focused on reentry support for individuals leaving prison, evaluations show that participants have significantly lower recidivism rates compared to the state average, suggesting that community understanding and support play a role in reducing repeat offenses.

Empathy-based initiatives are also measured by how well they mobilize community action. Community-led reform movements, participation in restorative justice practices, and advocacy for policy changes are all signs that empathy training has taken root within a population. Measuring the broader social impact of these initiatives can involve analyzing public sentiment through polls, media coverage, and policy shifts in favor of more compassionate justice practices.

While the data available is still emerging, initial studies suggest that empathy-based programs contribute to a more rehabilitative and supportive community environment. By measuring both individual and community-level changes, Florida and other states can continue to refine and expand these initiatives to create a more inclusive and empathetic society.

Chapter 19:
Resilience in the Face of Adversity

Resilience is the ability to adapt and bounce back when faced with challenges, adversity, or hardship. For incarcerated fathers, adversity takes many forms—separation from family, the stigma of incarceration, lack of access to meaningful rehabilitation, and the struggle to maintain a sense of identity and purpose while behind bars. These fathers face the dual challenge of navigating the prison system while trying to maintain relationships with their children and families from a distance. This requires an extraordinary level of resilience, not just for their own survival, but also to fulfill their role as fathers in a way that is supportive and beneficial for their children.

Building resilience is critical for incarcerated individuals because it directly influences their ability to cope with the stress and challenges of life in prison, as well as their eventual reentry into society. Resilience equips them to deal with the emotional toll of incarceration, but it also positions them to make the most of rehabilitative opportunities, such as educational programs, vocational training, and restorative justice initiatives. For incarcerated fathers, resilience is intertwined with their identity as caregivers and role models. This makes cultivating resilience not just a personal goal, but also a responsibility toward their families.

Identifying and Cultivating Resilience Among Incarcerated Fathers

Identifying and fostering resilience in incarcerated fathers starts with recognizing the unique set of emotional, psychological, and social challenges they face. These fathers are not only dealing with the personal consequences of their actions but are also grappling with the pain of separation from their children and the desire to maintain or rebuild family relationships. Many incarcerated fathers feel a deep sense of guilt and failure in their role as a parent, which can become a source of motivation to change, but can also be emotionally paralyzing. Recognizing this guilt as an opportunity for growth is one way to begin identifying resilience.

In Florida, several programs have been developed to cultivate resilience among incarcerated fathers, focusing on parenting skills, personal development, and emotional regulation. One such program is the Inside Out Dads initiative, which is implemented in prisons across the state. This program teaches fathers how to reconnect with their children, develop emotional resilience, and manage the stressors of incarceration. By focusing on the importance of fatherhood, these programs provide incarcerated men with a sense of purpose, which strengthens their resolve to transform their lives.

Resilience also develops through structured programs that offer emotional and psychological support. Incarcerated fathers who participate in cognitive-behavioral therapy (CBT) or mindfulness training often report better emotional regulation, lower levels of depression, and improved relationships with their families. These therapies help individuals confront their trauma, past mistakes, and internal struggles in a constructive way, allowing them to develop the mental strength required to persevere through difficult times. CBT, in particular, is designed to change negative thought patterns and cultivate healthier ways of responding to adversity. Studies show that individuals who undergo CBT while incarcerated are more likely to engage in positive coping strategies, making them less likely to reoffend after release.

Group-based interventions are also essential in identifying and cultivating resilience. Peer support groups, like those organized by the Florida Department of Corrections, provide a space for incarcerated fathers to share their experiences, challenges, and strategies for coping with the pressures of prison life. These support groups allow individuals to see that they are not alone in their struggles and encourage them to draw strength from the resilience of others. Listening to and learning from peers who have faced similar challenges helps incarcerated fathers realize that they, too, have the capacity for growth and change.

In addition to psychological interventions, resilience is also cultivated through practical support. Programs that provide vocational training, education, and skill-building help incarcerated fathers prepare for life after prison. The ability to envision a productive future outside of incarceration is a crucial element of resilience, and these programs offer fathers the tools to build that future. Florida's Ready4Work program, for example, offers incarcerated fathers job training, mentorship, and post-release support, which strengthens their resilience by giving them a sense of control over their lives and futures.

Lastly, resilience among incarcerated fathers is closely linked to their ability to maintain relationships with their children and families. Visitation programs, virtual calls, and letter-writing campaigns help fathers stay connected to their loved ones, giving them a reason to remain hopeful and committed to positive change. Fathers who feel supported by their families are often more resilient in the face of adversity, as the desire to reunite and provide for their children can serve as a powerful motivator.

By identifying the emotional, psychological, and practical needs of incarcerated fathers, programs in Florida and beyond can help these men cultivate the resilience they need to navigate the challenges of prison life and prepare for successful reentry into society.

Providing mentorship and support programs for incarcerated fathers is a critical component in fostering resilience and promoting successful reintegration into society. These programs serve as a bridge between incarceration and the challenges of reentry, offering guidance, resources, and emotional support. The value of mentorship lies not only in the practical skills imparted but also in the positive relationships formed, which can significantly influence the attitudes and behaviors of incarcerated individuals.

Mentorship programs tailored for incarcerated fathers can take various forms, from one-on-one mentoring relationships to group-based initiatives. These programs typically involve trained volunteers or community members who work directly with fathers in prison to help them develop crucial life skills, emotional intelligence, and parenting techniques. One successful model in Florida is the Children of Incarcerated Parents Project, which connects incarcerated fathers with mentors who have either experienced incarceration themselves or who have expertise in family dynamics and child development. These mentors provide guidance on how to maintain meaningful relationships with their children, manage emotions, and cultivate a sense of responsibility.

The process of mentoring not only benefits the incarcerated fathers but also has positive ripple effects on their families. Mentors can help fathers understand the emotional needs of their children and how to communicate effectively with them, even from a distance. This is particularly important for fathers who may feel disconnected or alienated from their families due to their incarceration. Through mentorship, these fathers can learn to navigate the complexities of fatherhood while incarcerated, including how to express love and care in ways that resonate with their children.

Support programs often include workshops that cover a range of topics relevant to incarcerated fathers. These may include parenting skills, conflict resolution, emotional regulation, and coping strategies for dealing with the stressors of prison life. For example, the Inside Out Dads program mentioned earlier incorporates mentorship elements by pairing incarcerated fathers with community mentors who guide them through the challenges of being a dad while in prison. By participating in these workshops, fathers not only gain essential skills but also build a sense of community and belonging, reducing feelings of isolation.

Moreover, providing access to educational and vocational training programs enhances the effectiveness of mentorship. In Florida, programs like Ready4Work and Pathways to Success offer inmates opportunities to gain skills that are marketable in the workforce. Mentors play a crucial role in these programs by helping fathers set realistic career goals, navigate job searches, and prepare for interviews. This comprehensive approach empowers incarcerated fathers to envision a future where they can be both responsible parents and productive members of society.

Peer mentoring, where formerly incarcerated individuals mentor those currently serving time, has proven particularly effective. These mentors bring lived experience, which fosters trust and relatability. Many incarcerated fathers are more likely to listen to and learn from someone who has faced similar struggles. Programs that utilize peer mentors often experience higher engagement rates and lower recidivism rates. The Florida Second Chance Initiative is an example of such a program, linking individuals who have successfully reintegrated into society with those still in the system.

Mentorship and support programs also extend beyond the prison walls. Successful reentry requires continued support from mentors and community organizations after release. Many programs provide a continuum of care, helping fathers transition back into their communities by connecting them with housing assistance, job training, and mental health services. This ongoing support is essential for helping fathers maintain their resilience and avoid the pitfalls that can lead to recidivism.

Family involvement is another vital aspect of mentorship programs. Involving family members in the process can strengthen familial bonds and create a support network that encourages positive behavior changes. Programs that facilitate family visits, virtual interactions, or workshops for families help reinforce the importance of maintaining relationships during incarceration. When fathers can see their families actively participating in their growth and development, it creates a powerful motivation to succeed and overcome adversity.

Ultimately, mentorship and support programs tailored for incarcerated fathers play a crucial role in promoting resilience, teaching valuable life skills, and fostering meaningful relationships. By addressing the unique challenges these fathers face, such programs not only benefit the individuals involved but also contribute to healthier families and communities.

Peer support and shared experiences play a vital role in the rehabilitation and reintegration of incarcerated fathers. These elements foster a sense of community, reduce feelings of isolation, and create an environment where individuals can learn from one another. In the context of incarceration, where emotional and psychological challenges are prevalent, peer support becomes an invaluable resource for fostering resilience and promoting positive change.

Incarcerated individuals often face stigma and alienation, both from society and within the prison environment. This isolation can exacerbate feelings of hopelessness and despair, making it difficult for them to envision a better future. Peer support groups offer a safe space where incarcerated fathers can express their thoughts, fears, and aspirations without judgment. By sharing their experiences, they create a sense of solidarity that helps individuals realize they are not alone in their struggles. This shared understanding fosters a supportive environment, encouraging members to share coping strategies and insights that can aid in personal growth.

Programs that emphasize peer support have shown to be particularly effective in enhancing the emotional well-being of incarcerated fathers. For example, the Inside Out Dad program encourages fathers to connect with one another through structured group sessions. These sessions focus on parenting skills, emotional regulation, and life planning, allowing fathers to draw strength from each other's experiences. Participants often find that discussing their challenges openly with peers who understand their circumstances leads to a greater sense of empowerment and hope.

Moreover, peer support can play a crucial role in mitigating the psychological effects of trauma. Many incarcerated individuals have experienced various forms of trauma—such as violence, abuse, or loss—which can significantly impact their mental health. By sharing their stories within a peer support framework, individuals can begin to process their trauma in a healthier way. This communal approach to healing helps them develop resilience and emotional strength, reducing the likelihood of mental health issues such as depression or anxiety.

The impact of peer support extends beyond emotional healing; it also contributes to personal accountability and motivation. When incarcerated fathers see their peers making positive changes—whether it be through educational achievements, personal development, or maintaining healthy family connections—they are inspired to pursue similar goals. This mutual motivation fosters an environment where individuals hold each other accountable, encouraging each other to stay focused on their rehabilitation and personal growth. The success stories shared within these groups can serve as powerful examples of what is possible, instilling hope and determination among participants.

Furthermore, peer support systems help individuals develop critical social skills that are essential for successful reentry into society. Many incarcerated fathers struggle with communication, conflict resolution, and relationship-building skills due to their experiences prior to and during incarceration. Engaging with peers in a supportive environment allows individuals to practice these skills in a low-pressure setting. They learn how to articulate their feelings, navigate interpersonal conflicts, and build trust—skills that are vital when they reintegrate into their families and communities.

Peer support can also provide practical assistance. Many incarcerated individuals benefit from learning about available resources for reentry, such as job training programs, educational opportunities, and mental health services. Peers who have successfully navigated these systems can offer invaluable insights and guidance, helping others to find their footing. This practical knowledge is often more relatable and easier to digest than information provided by professionals who may not share the same life experiences.

The importance of shared experiences is further highlighted when considering the specific challenges faced by incarcerated fathers. These individuals often grapple with feelings of guilt and shame regarding their roles as parents. By connecting with peers who share similar experiences of fatherhood, they can explore these emotions in a supportive context. Conversations that revolve around parenting—whether discussing strategies for maintaining connections with children or coping with the emotional weight of separation—allow incarcerated fathers to process their feelings and regain a sense of agency in their parenting roles.

In Florida, programs that leverage peer support among incarcerated fathers have shown promising results. For instance, community organizations often facilitate workshops where fathers can meet regularly, share their challenges, and collaborate on finding solutions. These interactions not only help fathers cope with their current situations but also prepare them for the complexities of life after release. By emphasizing the power of peer support and shared experiences, these programs contribute significantly to the overall goal of rehabilitation and successful reentry into society.

Building Resilience in the Face of Reentry Challenges

Reentry into society after incarceration presents a unique set of challenges that can test even the most resilient individuals. For incarcerated fathers, the transition back to family life, employment, and community involvement can be fraught with obstacles, including stigma, lack of resources, and emotional turmoil. Building resilience in the face of these challenges is crucial for successful reintegration and for maintaining their roles as fathers.

One of the most significant barriers to successful reentry is the stigma associated with incarceration. Many individuals face prejudice from employers, landlords, and even community members, making it difficult to secure stable housing and employment. This stigma can lead to feelings of hopelessness and isolation, which, in turn, undermine resilience. To combat this, support programs can play a vital role in empowering individuals with the tools they need to navigate these societal barriers. Programs that focus on self-advocacy and education about rights can help formerly incarcerated individuals understand and articulate their needs in a society that may not readily accept them.

A crucial aspect of building resilience involves equipping incarcerated fathers with practical skills that enhance their employability. Programs that provide vocational training, resume workshops, and interview preparation are essential in helping these men become competitive job candidates. In Florida, initiatives like the **Ready4Work** program offer not only job training but also connect individuals with employers who are open to hiring people with criminal records. This dual approach of skill development and networking helps fathers regain confidence and reinforces their sense of agency, which is essential for resilience.

Family dynamics also play a significant role in the resilience of incarcerated fathers during reentry. Many fathers struggle with the emotional fallout of their absence and fear how their families will receive them upon release. Rebuilding trust and relationships with their children and partners can be daunting but is necessary for their emotional well-being. Programs that facilitate family reunification—such as family counseling and parenting workshops—can provide a supportive framework for addressing these issues. In Florida, the **Family Reunification Program** focuses on helping incarcerated parents prepare for reentry through family-centered approaches, ensuring that fathers are equipped to rebuild relationships with their children.

Moreover, mental health support is crucial for resilience. Many incarcerated fathers have experienced trauma, which can resurface during the transition back to society. Access to mental health services—whether through therapy, support groups, or counseling—is vital for addressing these challenges. Trauma-informed care that recognizes the unique experiences of incarcerated individuals can help them develop coping strategies that are essential for navigating the stresses of reentry. Programs that provide ongoing mental health support help fathers manage anxiety, depression, and other mental health issues, fostering a greater sense of stability as they re-enter their communities.

Social support networks also significantly enhance resilience during reentry. The importance of peer connections cannot be overstated; having a support system of individuals who understand the challenges of reentry can provide both emotional and practical assistance. Peer mentorship programs, where formerly incarcerated individuals guide those recently released, can help new returnees navigate resources and make informed choices. The **Florida Second Chance Initiative** emphasizes peer mentoring, allowing individuals to share their experiences and offer support to one another, fostering a sense of belonging and community.

In addition to social support, community engagement is crucial for building resilience. Incarcerated fathers benefit from programs that encourage them to become involved in community service or local initiatives. Such involvement not only helps to rebuild their sense of purpose but also combats stigma by demonstrating their commitment to positive change. Programs that connect returning citizens with volunteer opportunities or community organizations can help fathers develop new skills, form meaningful relationships, and contribute positively to society.

Financial literacy is another key component in building resilience. Many formerly incarcerated individuals face significant economic challenges, from managing debts accrued during incarceration to navigating the complexities of budgeting. Workshops that focus on financial management, saving, and understanding credit can empower fathers to take control of their financial futures. This newfound knowledge can be empowering, as financial stability is often linked to a greater sense of overall well-being and resilience.

Finally, the role of hope in resilience should not be overlooked. Incarcerated fathers who can envision a better future for themselves and their families are more likely to persevere through challenges. Programs that focus on goal-setting and vision planning encourage individuals to define their aspirations and develop actionable steps toward achieving them. This forward-looking perspective instills a sense of purpose and motivation, reinforcing their ability to overcome obstacles.

By addressing the multifaceted challenges faced during reentry, and providing comprehensive support through mentorship, family engagement, mental health services, and skills training, programs can help incarcerated fathers build the resilience necessary to thrive after incarceration. The journey of reentry is undoubtedly challenging, but with the right support systems in place, these fathers can navigate their path toward successful reintegration, reclaim their roles in their families, and contribute positively to their communities.

Chapter 20
Learning from the Past, Shaping the Future

In the ongoing struggle to reform the criminal justice system, the importance of learning from past mistakes cannot be overstated. As society continues to evolve, so too must our understanding of crime, incarceration, and the pathways that lead individuals into the justice system. The failures and successes of the past provide invaluable lessons for shaping a more effective and humane system moving forward. By analyzing the root causes of crime, implementing evidence-based policies, and investing in prevention and intervention strategies, we can move beyond punitive approaches and focus on building a more equitable and restorative system. In this chapter, we explore how these key factors can drive lasting change and ensure a brighter future for individuals, families, and communities.

Understanding the root causes of crime and incarceration is critical to shaping effective policies that reduce recidivism, improve community safety, and offer better outcomes for both individuals and society as a whole. Analyzing these causes reveals that crime and incarceration are often influenced by a complex interplay of socioeconomic, psychological, and systemic factors. By identifying these underlying issues, we can begin to address the structural problems that lead individuals down the path of criminal behavior.

One of the most significant contributors to crime and subsequent incarceration is poverty. Individuals who grow up in impoverished environments are often exposed to higher levels of stress, instability, and limited access to resources. Poverty can lead to a lack of education, limited job opportunities, and unstable living conditions, all of which increase the likelihood of criminal involvement. In particular, youth from low-income neighborhoods may engage in criminal behavior as a means of survival or due to a lack of alternative opportunities. Research shows that areas with high poverty rates tend to have higher crime rates, particularly for violent crimes and property-related offenses. Addressing economic inequality is therefore a fundamental aspect of reducing crime rates.

Another significant root cause is inequality in education. Many individuals who become involved in the criminal justice system have a history of undereducation or lack access to quality schooling. Educational disparities are closely linked to socioeconomic status, with schools in underfunded areas often lacking the resources necessary to provide students with a supportive and effective learning environment. Low levels of educational attainment increase the risk of criminal behavior, as individuals with limited education face significant barriers to finding stable and legal employment. Programs that promote equal access to education, vocational training, and skill development have been shown to reduce crime rates by equipping individuals with the tools they need to build a productive future.

Family dynamics also play a key role in determining an individual's likelihood of becoming involved in criminal activity. Growing up in a family with high levels of dysfunction, such as substance abuse, domestic violence, or parental incarceration, can have a profound impact on a child's development. Children who experience trauma or neglect in their formative years are more likely to exhibit behavioral issues, which can lead to involvement in criminal activity later in life. Incarceration itself often perpetuates this cycle, as children of incarcerated parents are statistically more likely to become involved with the criminal justice system. Strengthening family support systems and providing resources for at-risk families can be an essential component of crime prevention.

Substance abuse and mental health issues are also closely tied to criminal behavior. A significant portion of individuals who are incarcerated struggle with substance abuse disorders, which often drive criminal actions such as theft, assault, or drug-related offenses. Additionally, mental health disorders, including depression, anxiety, and post-traumatic stress disorder (PTSD), can impair judgment and lead to decisions that result in criminal activity. Individuals with untreated mental health issues are disproportionately represented in the criminal justice system, underscoring the importance of providing adequate mental health care both inside and outside of correctional facilities.

Beyond individual and social factors, systemic issues within the criminal justice system itself also contribute to high incarceration rates. The "War on Drugs," which began in the 1980s, led to mass incarceration, particularly of people of color, for non-violent drug offenses. Harsh sentencing laws, mandatory minimums, and "three strikes" policies disproportionately affect minority communities and contribute to the overcrowding of prisons. Racial bias in policing, judicial sentencing, and law enforcement practices further exacerbates this issue, creating a cycle where certain communities are targeted and overrepresented in the prison population. Understanding and addressing these systemic injustices is key to reducing the overall rates of incarceration.

Recidivism is another critical issue that stems from both individual and systemic factors. Many individuals who are released from prison find themselves trapped in a cycle of reoffending due to a lack of support, employment opportunities, and reintegration services. Without stable housing, access to mental health care, or the ability to find legal employment, former inmates are often forced back into environments that perpetuate criminal behavior. Addressing recidivism requires not only criminal justice reform but also robust community-based support systems that help individuals successfully reintegrate into society after incarceration.

Finally, it's important to consider the role of community disinvestment in fostering conditions that lead to crime. Communities that lack access to healthcare, affordable housing, job opportunities, and social services are more likely to experience higher crime rates. By reinvesting in these underserved communities—creating jobs, improving schools, and expanding access to social services—we can help alleviate the conditions that contribute to criminal behavior and incarceration.

The importance of evidence-based policies in criminal justice reform cannot be overstated. By grounding policies in research and proven methodologies, we move toward a more equitable, effective, and humane justice system. Evidence-based practices focus on interventions that have been tested, measured, and proven to work in reducing crime, recidivism, and the negative impact of incarceration on individuals and communities. In contrast to outdated, punitive approaches that focus primarily on punishment, evidence-based strategies emphasize rehabilitation, prevention, and reintegration, offering solutions that benefit both society and the individuals within the system.

What Are Evidence-Based Policies?

Evidence-based policies rely on empirical data and research to inform decision-making. These policies use a systematic approach to analyze what works and what doesn't, based on results from past and ongoing programs. By evaluating the effectiveness of different interventions and collecting data on outcomes, evidence-based policies ensure that resources are allocated to programs with a demonstrated ability to reduce crime and improve rehabilitation.

In the context of criminal justice, evidence-based policies encompass a range of practices designed to address the underlying causes of criminal behavior, promote rehabilitation, and reduce recidivism. Programs such as cognitive-behavioral therapy (CBT), substance abuse treatment, vocational training, and education within prisons have been rigorously studied and shown to produce measurable improvements in the lives of incarcerated individuals and their families. For example, CBT programs help individuals recognize and change the thought patterns that lead to criminal behavior, offering long-term solutions for breaking the cycle of reoffending.

Traditional approaches to crime and punishment have often focused on deterrence through incarceration and harsh sentencing laws, such as mandatory minimums and three-strikes laws. However, these methods have not only failed to reduce crime rates significantly, but they have also contributed to the overcrowding of prisons and the disproportionate incarceration of people from marginalized communities. In response, evidence-based policies seek to shift the focus from punitive measures to rehabilitative and restorative practices that address the root causes of crime.

For example, restorative justice programs—such as victim-offender mediation—have been found to reduce reoffending rates by fostering empathy, accountability, and healing between the victim and the offender. Similarly, diversion programs for non-violent offenders, which emphasize treatment over incarceration, have proven effective in addressing issues like substance abuse and mental health, which are common among individuals in the criminal justice system.

The Role of Data in Policymaking

Data is the cornerstone of evidence-based policy. Without data, policymakers cannot determine which interventions are successful or identify areas that need improvement. By analyzing recidivism rates, behavioral changes, and other key indicators, researchers can identify patterns and design interventions that address the specific needs of different populations within the justice system.

For example, recidivism data has shown that individuals who participate in vocational training and educational programs while incarcerated are significantly less likely to reoffend upon release. This data has informed the expansion of prison education programs across the United States, ensuring that incarcerated individuals have the skills and knowledge needed to successfully reintegrate into society.

Moreover, data-driven approaches help to highlight disparities within the system, such as racial and socioeconomic inequalities. By examining the ways in which certain populations are disproportionately affected by the criminal justice system, policymakers can develop targeted interventions that promote fairness and justice. This ensures that resources are directed toward the communities and individuals who need them most, rather than applying a one-size-fits-all solution.

One powerful example of the effectiveness of evidence-based policies is the success of drug courts. Drug courts offer a therapeutic alternative to incarceration for individuals with substance abuse disorders, combining treatment and rehabilitation with strict oversight and accountability. Studies have shown that drug courts significantly reduce recidivism rates compared to traditional sentencing, as participants receive the support they need to overcome addiction while also facing clear consequences for non-compliance. Drug courts not only benefit individuals by breaking the cycle of addiction and crime but also reduce the burden on the prison system and save taxpayer money.

Similarly, the HOPE (Hawaii's Opportunity Probation with Enforcement) program in Hawaii has been praised for its evidence-based approach to probation. The program focuses on swift, certain, and proportionate responses to probation violations, rather than lengthy incarceration. Participants are held accountable for their actions but are also provided with the resources and support necessary to succeed in the community. Research has shown that individuals in the HOPE program are less likely to re-offend and more likely to complete their probation successfully.

One of the key strengths of evidence-based policies is their adaptability. As new research emerges and as society's understanding of crime evolves, policies can be adjusted to reflect current knowledge and best practices. This flexibility ensures that the criminal justice system can respond effectively to emerging challenges, such as the opioid crisis, the growing need for mental health services, and the demand for criminal justice reform.

Evidence-based policies also encourage innovation within the system. By fostering a culture of continuous learning and improvement, policymakers can experiment with new approaches and evaluate their effectiveness before scaling them up. This process of trial and evaluation is crucial for ensuring that the justice system evolves in response to changing social, economic, and cultural conditions.

While the benefits of evidence-based policies are clear, implementing these approaches on a large scale presents several challenges. One of the primary obstacles is the resistance to change within the criminal justice system, particularly among policymakers and law enforcement officials who may be skeptical of new approaches. Additionally, funding for evidence-based programs can be limited, particularly in states with tight budgets or political climates that favor punitive approaches.

To overcome these challenges, it is essential to build strong coalitions of stakeholders, including policymakers, criminal justice professionals, advocates, and community members, who support the implementation of evidence-based policies. By raising awareness of the proven benefits of these approaches, advocates can help to shift public opinion and generate the political will needed to enact meaningful reform.

Investing in Prevention and Early Intervention Programs

Investing in prevention and early intervention programs is a critical strategy for reducing crime and incarceration rates while promoting long-term public safety. These programs aim to address the root causes of criminal behavior, such as poverty, trauma, lack of education, and mental health issues, by providing support and resources before individuals come into contact with the criminal justice system. Early intervention is a proactive approach that helps divert individuals away from pathways leading to crime and incarceration, ensuring that communities are strengthened rather than weakened by these systemic issues.

Early intervention is crucial because it targets the factors that contribute to criminal behavior, especially among at-risk youth and vulnerable populations. Studies show that individuals who face adverse childhood experiences (ACEs), such as abuse, neglect, or exposure to violence, are at a significantly higher risk of engaging in criminal activity later in life. By investing in programs that address these issues early on, society can prevent many individuals from entering the criminal justice system in the first place.

For example, programs that focus on improving parenting skills, providing mental health services, and offering substance abuse prevention can have a profound impact on families and communities. In many cases, crime is the result of unmet needs—whether those needs are for emotional support, financial stability, or health services. Early intervention programs seek to meet those needs, thereby reducing the likelihood that individuals will turn to crime as a means of coping with their circumstances.

One of the most effective forms of early intervention is investment in education. Research consistently shows that individuals with higher levels of education are less likely to be involved in the criminal justice system. School-based programs, such as mentorship initiatives, after-school programs, and conflict

141

resolution training, can help keep young people engaged in their education and away from negative influences that could lead to criminal behavior.

Programs like "Communities In Schools" (CIS), which is active in Florida and other states, focus on providing support for at-risk students to help them succeed academically and stay in school. By offering tutoring, counseling, and resources for basic needs, CIS works to remove the barriers that often prevent students from reaching their full potential. The success of these programs demonstrates that early intervention in education can have a long-term positive effect on reducing dropout rates, which are often correlated with higher rates of criminal activity.

Another key area for prevention and early intervention is mental health and substance abuse treatment. Many individuals who end up in the criminal justice system suffer from untreated mental health conditions or addiction. In fact, the National Alliance on Mental Illness (NAMI) reports that approximately 44% of jail inmates have been diagnosed with a mental health disorder. Early identification and treatment of these issues can prevent escalation into criminal behavior.

Programs that provide mental health screenings, counseling, and access to treatment services can intervene before individuals reach a crisis point that could lead to criminal activity. Substance abuse prevention programs, such as those that educate individuals about the risks of drug use and offer rehabilitation services, also play a significant role in reducing crime rates. For example, Florida's Department of Children and Families has implemented prevention programs targeting substance use among youth, aiming to educate them early on about the dangers of drug addiction. These programs help steer young people away from behaviors that could lead to arrest and incarceration.

Community-based prevention programs are essential in addressing the social and economic conditions that contribute to crime. These programs work at the local level to provide resources, build social networks, and strengthen community ties, all of which help reduce crime rates. Initiatives such as community policing, neighborhood watch programs, and gang intervention efforts engage residents in creating safer, more cohesive communities.

For example, Operation Peacemaker Fellowship, which originated in Richmond, California, but could serve as a model for Florida, provides mentorship and support to individuals at high risk of committing violent crimes. Participants in the program receive job training, education, and counseling, as well as financial support to help them transition away from criminal activity. By focusing on prevention and providing alternatives to violence, the program has seen significant reductions in crime rates within the communities it serves.

Addressing economic disparities is another essential component of crime prevention. Poverty and lack of economic opportunity are closely linked to criminal behavior, particularly in communities that have been historically marginalized. Investing in job training programs, affordable housing, and other social services can reduce the economic pressures that contribute to crime.

Programs that provide vocational training and job placement services for individuals in high-risk communities have been shown to reduce criminal activity. These programs offer participants the skills and resources they need to secure stable employment, which is one of the most effective ways to prevent future criminal behavior. By investing in the economic well-being of communities, policymakers can create environments where individuals are less likely to turn to crime out of desperation or lack of opportunity.

Investing in prevention and early intervention programs is not only effective in reducing crime but also cost-efficient. The cost of incarceration is far higher than the cost of preventive measures. According to the Vera Institute of Justice, the average cost of incarcerating an individual in the U.S. is approximately $31,000 per year[10]. In contrast, prevention programs that provide mental health services, substance abuse treatment, and educational support can be funded at a fraction of the cost and produce long-lasting benefits.

Florida, for example, has taken steps to implement juvenile justice diversion programs, which offer alternatives to incarceration for young offenders. These programs focus on rehabilitation and education rather than punishment and have been shown to reduce recidivism rates significantly. By diverting individuals from the criminal justice system early on, these programs save the state money while promoting public safety and individual well-being.

Data-Driven Policymaking and Evaluation

Data-driven policymaking is the practice of using empirical evidence, statistical data, and analytical insights to inform the creation, implementation, and evaluation of policies, particularly in the criminal justice system. This approach seeks to improve policy outcomes by grounding decisions in verifiable data rather than intuition, tradition, or political ideology. When applied effectively, data-driven policymaking can lead to more efficient use of resources, more equitable justice outcomes, and an overall reduction in crime and recidivism rates.

In the context of criminal justice, data-driven policymaking is crucial for understanding the true impact of various laws, policies, and programs. It allows legislators, law enforcement, and correctional institutions to assess what is working and what is not,

---

[10] https://www.vera.org/publications/price-of-prisons-what-incarceration-costs-taxpayers

identify trends in crime and incarceration, and make adjustments accordingly.

One major benefit of data-driven policymaking is that it facilitates evidence-based reforms. Rather than relying on assumptions, stakeholders can examine historical data, real-time statistics, and predictive analytics to inform decisions that are most likely to succeed. This method can highlight both areas where the system is functioning well and areas where changes need to be made. It also helps in setting measurable goals, tracking progress, and making informed decisions that lead to meaningful improvements.

For instance, research shows that focusing resources on rehabilitation and reintegration programs for inmates can lead to significant reductions in recidivism rates. By tracking recidivism data and analyzing which programs are most effective in reducing repeat offenses, states like Florida can adjust their criminal justice policies to prioritize methods that show positive outcomes.

Data can be used at multiple stages of the policymaking process, from the identification of problems to the development of solutions and the evaluation of their impact. This cyclical process ensures that policies remain relevant, effective, and responsive to the needs of the community.

1. **Problem Identification:** Data collection allows for a clearer understanding of the root causes of issues within the criminal justice system. For example, statistics on incarceration rates, demographics, crime trends, and sentencing disparities can reveal systemic problems, such as racial inequalities, over-incarceration, or the failure of certain types of sentencing to deter crime. Data might show that non-violent offenders are incarcerated at disproportionately high rates or that certain communities are over-policed, prompting calls for reforms in sentencing laws or policing practices.

2. **Solution Development:** Once the problem has been clearly identified through data analysis, policymakers can begin crafting solutions that directly address these issues. Data on effective interventions, such as rehabilitation programs, mental health support, and diversion initiatives, can guide the creation of policies that focus on reducing criminal behavior rather than simply punishing it. Evidence from states that have successfully implemented reforms can be a powerful tool for shaping new approaches in other areas.

3. **Policy Implementation and Monitoring:** After a policy is implemented, continuous data collection allows for monitoring its impact. Key performance indicators (KPIs) such as recidivism rates, crime rates, and community engagement can be tracked to evaluate whether the policy is having the desired effect. For example, Florida's use of the Justice Reinvestment Initiative (JRI) relies on data-driven monitoring to allocate resources more effectively, reduce prison populations, and invest in community programs. By examining ongoing data, policymakers can tweak or overhaul programs to improve their effectiveness.

4. **Evaluation and Adjustment**: Data-driven evaluation ensures that policies are adaptable. If data reveals that a particular approach isn't delivering the expected results, adjustments can be made. This iterative process fosters flexibility and responsiveness, helping policies evolve alongside changes in the population, economy, or social landscape.

One of the most valuable uses of data in criminal justice policymaking is the ability to evaluate the effectiveness of existing programs and policies. Rigorous data collection allows for comprehensive evaluations, leading to smarter decisions on whether to scale, modify, or discontinue a particular initiative.

In Florida, programs like the juvenile justice diversion initiative are prime examples of the value of data-driven evaluation. By tracking the outcomes of youth who participate in diversion programs compared to those who go through the traditional court system, officials can measure success in terms of recidivism, educational attainment, and overall community impact. If the data shows that diversion programs reduce recidivism, policymakers can expand them as a proven method to reduce juvenile crime.

Another example is the evaluation of the effectiveness of drug courts in addressing substance abuse-related offenses. Florida's drug courts are specialized programs that aim to divert non-violent drug offenders into treatment rather than incarceration. Data on relapse rates, successful completion of treatment programs, and subsequent criminal behavior can be analyzed to determine whether drug courts are achieving their goals. If the data shows positive outcomes, the state can allocate more resources to these programs or replicate their success in other areas.

While the benefits of data-driven policymaking are clear, there are also challenges. First, data collection must be accurate, comprehensive, and free from bias. Incomplete or biased data can lead to flawed conclusions and ineffective policies. Additionally, policymakers must have access to the right tools and expertise to analyze data effectively, which requires investment in training and technology.

Another challenge is ensuring transparency and accountability in how data is used. Policymakers must ensure that data-driven decisions are communicated clearly to the public and that there is accountability when policies do not meet their intended goals. This transparency helps build trust in the criminal justice system, particularly in communities that have historically been over-policed or disproportionately affected by incarceration.

Data must be continuously updated and analyzed to reflect changing social, economic, and legal conditions. Policymakers must be committed to making adjustments as new information becomes available and be willing to revise or abandon policies that are not delivering positive results.

The Role of Research and Evidence in Driving Change

Research and evidence play a critical role in shaping policies, driving reforms, and fostering change within the criminal justice system. Informed decision-making, based on rigorous research, ensures that the solutions implemented are not only theoretically sound but also effective in practice. Within the context of the criminal justice system, including Florida's initiatives, evidence-based approaches provide a reliable framework for addressing the complexities of crime, incarceration, and rehabilitation.

Evidence-based practices (EBPs) in the criminal justice system refer to the use of research findings and data to guide decision-making. These practices emphasize solutions that have been empirically tested and proven to be effective through comprehensive studies and trials. Whether it's rehabilitative programs for incarcerated individuals, law enforcement strategies, or sentencing reforms, evidence-based approaches ensure that the interventions being used are backed by scientific proof of their success.

By incorporating EBPs, states like Florida can make informed choices about which programs to fund, expand, or discontinue based on their proven effectiveness. For example, research into drug treatment programs for offenders has shown that certain approaches can significantly reduce recidivism. By using this research, policymakers can ensure that resources are allocated toward programs with the highest likelihood of reducing repeat offenses,

148

rather than relying on punitive measures that may be ineffective in the long term.

Research also helps identify the root causes of issues in the criminal justice system. Studies on crime trends, demographic data, and social factors contribute to a more nuanced understanding of why certain populations are disproportionately affected by crime and incarceration. For instance, research has consistently shown that systemic factors such as poverty, education, and community support are significant predictors of crime. By understanding these factors, Florida's policymakers can focus on addressing the underlying causes of criminal behavior rather than just its symptoms.

Moreover, research is critical in identifying racial and ethnic disparities within the system. Studies have shown that people of color, particularly Black and Latino communities, are disproportionately represented in prisons across the U.S., including Florida. This overrepresentation often stems from structural inequalities, biased policing practices, and unequal access to legal resources. By relying on research to shed light on these disparities, reformers can advocate for policy changes that address systemic racism within the criminal justice system.

Rigorous research and evaluation of existing programs are crucial for determining what works and what doesn't. In Florida, programs designed to rehabilitate offenders, such as drug courts, educational programs, and vocational training, are often evaluated to assess their success rates. These evaluations are typically based on metrics like recidivism rates, successful completion of programs, and long-term social reintegration outcomes.

For example, studies on Florida's drug courts have demonstrated their success in reducing recidivism among non-violent drug offenders. These courts focus on treatment rather than punishment, and the research has consistently shown that participants are less likely to re-offend after completing these programs. This evidence has led to the expansion of drug courts in the state and has encouraged the adoption of similar approaches for other non-violent offenses.

In contrast, programs that show limited success or fail to meet their objectives can be reformed or discontinued. For instance, research may reveal that certain punitive measures or long-term incarceration for low-level offenses do not deter crime and may actually contribute to higher rates of reoffending. Armed with this knowledge, policymakers can shift resources away from ineffective practices and toward more productive approaches.

Research is essential for advancing legislative reforms. Policymakers, advocates, and activists use data and research findings to push for evidence-based reforms that address the flaws within the criminal justice system. When lobbying for legislative change, stakeholders often present research findings to lawmakers to demonstrate the potential benefits of a proposed policy change or program. These findings provide a solid foundation for building bipartisan support for criminal justice reform initiatives.

For instance, research on the negative impact of mandatory minimum sentencing laws has been instrumental in efforts to reform these laws. Studies have shown that mandatory minimums contribute to mass incarceration without significantly reducing crime rates. This evidence has sparked discussions at both the state and federal levels, including in Florida, about the need for sentencing reform. As a result, some states have reduced or eliminated mandatory minimums for non-violent offenses, particularly drug-related crimes, with the goal of reducing prison populations and focusing more on rehabilitation.

Similarly, research on the effectiveness of early intervention programs, such as those targeting at-risk youth, has provided a strong rationale for increased investment in prevention efforts. By demonstrating the long-term benefits of these programs, including lower crime rates and reduced incarceration costs, advocates can push for policies that prioritize early intervention over punitive responses.

As the criminal justice landscape continues to evolve, ongoing research is necessary to keep up with emerging challenges. The rise of digital crime, the impact of opioid addiction, and the role of mental health in criminal behavior are just a few areas where additional research is needed to inform future policies.

Additionally, research is crucial for adapting to societal changes and shifts in public opinion. In recent years, there has been a growing recognition of the need for more humane and rehabilitative approaches to criminal justice, as opposed to punitive measures. Public support for reforms such as decriminalizing certain drug offenses, expanding parole opportunities, and providing mental health services has been bolstered by research showing the efficacy of these approaches.

Finally, research also plays a key role in ensuring accountability within the criminal justice system. Continuous monitoring and evaluation of policies and programs ensure that the system remains transparent, effective, and fair.

Research and evidence-based practices are the cornerstones of meaningful criminal justice reform. By relying on rigorous studies and data analysis, Florida and other states can implement policies that address the root causes of crime, reduce recidivism, and improve outcomes for both offenders and the broader community. As the criminal justice system faces new challenges, continued investment in research will be essential for shaping the future of justice in the United States.

Chapter 21
Empowering Voices of Change

Diversity and inclusion are essential components of a just and equitable society, particularly when addressing the pervasive and systemic issues within the criminal justice system. In recent years, there has been an increasing recognition that the justice system disproportionately impacts marginalized communities, particularly people of color. Incarceration rates for Black, Latino, and Indigenous populations remain significantly higher than those of white individuals, leading to long-lasting consequences for families and communities. Embracing diversity and inclusion within the criminal justice framework involves not only recognizing these disparities but actively working to dismantle the systems that perpetuate inequality. By promoting fairness, equity, and support for all individuals, particularly those from underrepresented and marginalized backgrounds, the justice system can begin to foster rehabilitation, healing, and long-term social change.

Addressing Racial Disparities in the Criminal Justice System

Racial disparities within the criminal justice system have been a well-documented and long-standing issue, particularly in states like Florida. Systemic inequalities lead to disproportionately higher rates of arrest, prosecution, and incarceration for people of color, especially Black and Latino individuals. Addressing these disparities requires acknowledging the complex web of factors that contribute to them, including biased policing, unequal access to legal resources, and sentencing policies that disproportionately affect minority communities.

In Florida, Black individuals make up around 17% of the state's population but account for nearly 47% of its prison population, underscoring the deep racial imbalances within the justice system. Many studies have shown that Black and Latino individuals are more likely to be arrested and incarcerated for drug-related offenses, even though drug use rates are similar across racial groups. Additionally, mandatory minimum sentencing laws and "three-strikes" policies have had a disproportionately negative impact on communities of color, often resulting in longer sentences for minor or non-violent offenses.

One contributing factor to racial disparities in the criminal justice system is racial profiling by law enforcement. This practice, whether intentional or implicit, leads to the over-policing of communities of color, creating a cycle of arrest and incarceration that is difficult to break. Racial profiling also results in higher rates of stops, searches, and arrests for Black and Latino individuals, even in cases where no crime has been committed. In Florida, for instance, Black drivers are more likely to be stopped and searched by law enforcement than white drivers, despite white drivers being more likely to be found with contraband.

Another critical factor is the lack of access to quality legal representation for many individuals from marginalized communities. Public defenders are often overworked and underfunded, leading to less effective defense strategies for those who cannot afford private attorneys. This disparity in legal representation disproportionately affects people of color, contributing to higher conviction rates and longer sentences. In many cases, individuals from low-income communities, who are often people of color, are pressured into accepting plea deals, even when they may be innocent or facing minor charges, simply because they cannot afford the lengthy and expensive process of going to trial.

Addressing these disparities requires a multi-faceted approach that includes legal reform, increased oversight of law enforcement practices, and greater access to resources for individuals from marginalized communities. One important step is the reform of sentencing laws that disproportionately impact people of color. Florida, like many other states, has begun to re-examine its mandatory minimum sentencing laws, particularly for non-violent drug offenses, in an effort to reduce racial disparities in incarceration rates. By eliminating or reducing mandatory minimums for certain offenses, the state can help ensure that individuals are sentenced based on the specific circumstances of their cases, rather than being subjected to overly harsh and uniform penalties.

Additionally, improving access to legal representation for individuals from marginalized communities is crucial. Increasing funding for public defenders and legal aid services can help ensure that all individuals, regardless of their financial circumstances, receive a fair trial. Community-based organizations and legal advocacy groups can also play a role by providing support and resources to individuals who may otherwise be unable to navigate the complex legal system.

Education and training for law enforcement officers are another important strategy for addressing racial disparities in the justice system. Implicit bias training, for instance, can help officers recognize and address unconscious biases that may affect their decision-making. Additionally, increasing diversity within law enforcement agencies themselves can help build trust between officers and the communities they serve, particularly in communities of color where trust in law enforcement is often low due to historical and ongoing instances of racial profiling and police violence.

Efforts to address racial disparities in the criminal justice system must also involve a focus on reentry programs and the barriers that formerly incarcerated individuals, particularly people of color, face when reintegrating into society. Discriminatory hiring practices, housing discrimination, and other forms of systemic racism often make it difficult for individuals with criminal records to rebuild their lives after serving their sentences. Comprehensive reentry support programs that address these barriers are essential for reducing recidivism and promoting long-term rehabilitation.

Promoting Equity and Fairness in Reentry Programs

Reentry programs serve as a vital bridge for individuals transitioning from incarceration back into society. However, for these programs to be effective, they must be designed with equity and fairness at their core. This involves not only addressing the unique needs of individuals but also actively combating the systemic barriers that often hinder successful reintegration, particularly for marginalized communities.

Equity in reentry means providing individuals with the specific resources and support they need based on their unique circumstances, rather than a one-size-fits-all approach. For instance, individuals from different backgrounds may face varying challenges upon release, such as a lack of access to housing, employment opportunities, or social services. Acknowledging these differences is crucial in creating reentry programs that work for everyone.

To promote equity, reentry programs should offer tailored support services that consider the diverse backgrounds and experiences of individuals. This includes:

1. **Culturally Competent Services:** Programs should incorporate cultural competence in their services. Staff and facilitators must be trained to understand and respect the cultural backgrounds of the individuals they serve, ensuring that they can communicate effectively and build trust.

2. **Individualized Case Management:** Providing individualized case management can help address the specific barriers faced by each person. Case managers should work with individuals to create personalized plans that

consider their history, family dynamics, and community resources.

3. **Access to Mental Health and Substance Abuse Treatment:** Many individuals returning from incarceration have experienced trauma or may struggle with substance abuse. Access to mental health and substance use treatment should be integrated into reentry programs, providing comprehensive support that addresses both psychological and addiction issues.

Employment is a critical factor in successful reentry, yet many individuals face discrimination in the job market due to their criminal records. To promote equity in this area, reentry programs should:

1. **Build Partnerships with Employers:** Establishing partnerships with local businesses and organizations can create job opportunities specifically for individuals with criminal backgrounds. Programs can offer incentives for employers who are willing to hire these individuals, helping to reduce stigma and promote inclusivity.

2. **Provide Job Training and Skills Development:** Reentry programs should include job training and skills development that align with the needs of the local job market. This not only enhances employability but also gives individuals the confidence to seek and maintain employment.

3. **Advocate for Fair Chance Hiring Policies**: Advocacy for fair chance hiring policies at the local and state levels can help create a more equitable job market. These policies can reduce barriers for individuals with criminal records, ensuring they have a fair opportunity to secure employment.

Housing stability is another crucial component of successful reentry. Programs should work to ensure that individuals have access to safe and stable housing upon their release. This can involve:

1. **Housing Assistance Programs:** Providing assistance with finding and securing housing can greatly improve an individual's chances of success. This includes helping with applications, and deposits, and connecting individuals with supportive housing programs.

2. **Transitional Housing Options:** Offering transitional housing that provides a supportive environment for individuals can help ease the transition. These programs can provide structured support and resources while individuals establish themselves in the community.

3. **Support for Families:** Reentry programs should also consider the needs of individuals' families, recognizing that family dynamics can significantly impact the reentry process. Providing family support services can help to strengthen these relationships and promote stability.

To promote equity and fairness in reentry programs, continuous evaluation and improvement are essential. Programs should regularly assess their impact and effectiveness, collecting data to understand how well they are meeting the needs of diverse populations. This feedback loop can help identify gaps in services and inform necessary adjustments.

Diversity and Inclusion Training for Service Providers

Diversity and inclusion training for service providers is essential in fostering an equitable and just environment for individuals who have been incarcerated. This training equips professionals with the necessary tools, knowledge, and skills to effectively engage with diverse populations, ensuring that all individuals receive fair treatment and appropriate services as they navigate the complexities of reentry into society. In the context of criminal justice and reentry programs, such training can help dismantle systemic biases and promote culturally competent care.

The criminal justice system has historically been plagued by racial, ethnic, and socio-economic disparities. Service providers often work with individuals from various backgrounds, each with unique experiences and challenges. Therefore, understanding these differences is crucial in delivering effective support. Diversity and inclusion training serves multiple purposes:

1. **Awareness of Implicit Bias:** Training helps service providers recognize their own implicit biases, which can unconsciously influence their interactions with clients. By addressing these biases, providers can work towards minimizing their impact on decision-making and service delivery.

2. **Cultural Competence:** Understanding the cultural contexts of the individuals served is vital. Training enhances cultural competence, allowing providers to engage with clients respectfully and effectively, leading to better communication and trust.

3. **Improving Service Delivery:** Providers who are trained in diversity and inclusion can tailor their services to better meet the needs of diverse populations. This can lead to more successful outcomes for clients, as programs become more responsive to individual experiences and needs.

Key Components of Diversity and Inclusion Training

For diversity and inclusion training to be effective, it should encompass several key components:

1. **Education on Systemic Inequities:** Training should begin with an overview of systemic inequities within the criminal

justice system, including historical context, statistics, and personal narratives. This foundational knowledge helps service providers understand the broader landscape in which they operate.

2. **Skill Development:** Practical skills are essential for effective engagement with diverse populations. Training should include role-playing scenarios, case studies, and workshops that allow providers to practice culturally responsive techniques. This hands-on approach helps build confidence and competence in addressing real-world situations.

3. **Trauma-Informed Care:** Given the prevalence of trauma among individuals in the criminal justice system, integrating trauma-informed care principles into diversity and inclusion training is crucial. Providers should learn to recognize signs of trauma, understand its impacts, and apply trauma-informed practices that promote safety, trust, and empowerment.

4. **Promoting Allyship:** Training should encourage service providers to become allies in the fight for equity and justice. This includes understanding their role in advocating for systemic change and supporting the voices of those with lived experiences.

5. **Creating Inclusive Environments:** Providers should learn strategies for fostering inclusive environments within their organizations. This may involve developing policies that promote diversity, ensuring diverse representation in leadership roles, and creating support networks for marginalized staff and clients.

Implementing effective diversity and inclusion training involves a systematic approach:

1. **Needs Assessment:** Organizations should conduct assessments to identify specific areas where training is needed. Gathering feedback from staff and clients can provide valuable insights into the challenges faced and the areas for improvement.

2. **Collaboration with Experts:** Partnering with diversity and inclusion experts or organizations can enhance training programs. These experts can provide valuable resources, curriculum development, and facilitation skills that improve the quality of training.

3. **Continuous Learning:** Diversity and inclusion training should not be a one-time event but rather an ongoing process. Regularly scheduled training sessions, workshops, and discussions can help reinforce the principles of diversity and inclusion and keep staff engaged.

4. **Evaluation and Feedback:** Organizations should implement mechanisms for evaluating the effectiveness of their training programs. This can involve surveys, focus groups, and performance assessments to gauge the impact on service delivery and client satisfaction.

The benefits of diversity and inclusion training for service providers can be profound:

1. **Improved Relationships:** Trained providers are better equipped to build trusting relationships with clients, leading to more effective engagement and collaboration.

2. **Increased Accessibility:** By understanding the barriers faced by diverse populations, service providers can work to

create more accessible services that meet the unique needs of individuals from different backgrounds.

3. **Enhanced Outcomes:** Ultimately, diversity and inclusion training can lead to improved outcomes for individuals reentering society. By promoting equity and fairness, programs can contribute to breaking the cycle of incarceration and fostering successful reintegration.

In conclusion, diversity and inclusion training for service providers is a critical component of creating a more just and equitable criminal justice system. By equipping professionals with the skills and knowledge needed to engage effectively with diverse populations, we can promote fair treatment, enhance service delivery, and ultimately support the successful reentry of individuals into their communities.

Dismantling systemic racism in the criminal justice system requires a comprehensive, multi-faceted approach that addresses the underlying structures and practices perpetuating inequality. Systemic racism is not merely an issue of individual prejudice but is embedded within laws, policies, and institutional practices that disadvantage certain racial and ethnic groups. As such, it necessitates a collaborative effort from policymakers, community organizations, and individuals to promote equity and justice within the system.

One of the most effective strategies for dismantling systemic racism is advocating for comprehensive policy reform. This includes eliminating mandatory minimum sentences, which disproportionately impact communities of color. Reforming these laws can reduce the number of individuals incarcerated for non-violent offenses and allow for more equitable sentencing practices. Decriminalizing certain offenses, particularly those related to drug use and mental health, is another critical step. These offenses often disproportionately affect marginalized communities, and decriminalizing them can redirect individuals toward treatment and support services rather than punishment. Continuous assessment of current laws and policies for their impacts on racial disparities is crucial; engaging stakeholders, including affected communities, in these reviews can lead to more informed and equitable policy decisions.

Engaging communities directly affected by systemic racism is vital for developing effective strategies to combat it. Grassroots organizing can support movements advocating for criminal justice reform, amplifying the voices of marginalized communities. These movements often have firsthand experience with systemic issues and can propose actionable solutions. Community policing initiatives can also play a significant role in building trust between law enforcement and communities of color. By fostering collaboration and positive engagement, community policing can reduce tensions and improve relations. Additionally, providing education, resources, and training to communities can empower individuals to advocate for themselves and their rights. This can involve workshops on legal rights, navigating the criminal justice system, and community organizing.

For meaningful change to occur within the criminal justice system, law enforcement agencies must commit to anti-racism training and education. Implementing comprehensive training on implicit bias for police officers and other personnel can help them recognize and address their biases, ultimately leading to fairer treatment of all individuals. Training programs should also focus on cultural competency, equipping officers with the skills to understand and respect the diverse backgrounds of the communities they serve. Establishing clear accountability measures for law enforcement practices can help ensure that officers adhere to anti-racist principles. This includes implementing independent oversight bodies to investigate complaints of misconduct and racial profiling.

Redirecting resources from punitive measures to community-based alternatives can help dismantle systemic racism by addressing the root causes of crime. Supporting mental health and substance abuse treatment programs can enable individuals to receive the support they need rather than being funneled into the criminal justice system. Expanding educational and employment opportunities for marginalized communities can significantly reduce crime rates and contribute to community stability. Moreover, promoting restorative justice practices that prioritize healing and reconciliation over punishment can facilitate a more equitable system that acknowledges the harm caused to individuals and communities while fostering dialogue and understanding. By focusing on these comprehensive strategies, we can work toward dismantling the systemic racism entrenched in our criminal justice system and fostering a more equitable society for all.

Chapter 22
Bridging Divides, Building Trust

R ebuilding lives and communities after incarceration requires more than just policy reform; it calls for collaboration between various sectors to address the complex challenges faced by formerly incarcerated individuals. The chapter "Bridging Divides, Building Trust" focuses on creating partnerships and fostering collaboration among government entities, community organizations, and the private sector to develop comprehensive reentry strategies. Effective reentry programs require support across different fields, as each sector has a unique role in addressing the social, economic, and structural barriers faced by individuals returning to society after imprisonment.

One of the most significant ways to build sustainable reentry efforts is through collaboration between government agencies, community organizations, and the private sector. Each of these stakeholders plays a pivotal role in creating a safety net for formerly incarcerated individuals, ensuring they receive the support and opportunities they need to reintegrate successfully.

Government agencies, particularly those at the state and local levels, have the capacity to develop policies that facilitate reentry. They can create the framework within which reentry programs operate, ensuring that those leaving the prison system have access to necessary services such as mental health support, job training, housing assistance, and legal aid. For example, Florida's Department of Corrections has implemented programs that partner with community-based organizations to provide wrap-around services for returning citizens. These programs often work in tandem with parole and probation services, ensuring continuity of care from prison to community.

At the same time, community organizations, especially those based in the neighborhoods most affected by incarceration, have an intimate understanding of the challenges and needs of individuals returning from prison. These organizations are often staffed by individuals who have been through the justice system themselves or have lived in communities impacted by mass incarceration. This lived experience allows community organizations to provide more personalized, culturally competent services. For instance, non-profits like Florida Rights Restoration Coalition (FRRC) work directly with returning citizens, providing not only legal assistance but also help with voter rights restoration and community reintegration. They are vital in creating community-led solutions that reflect the actual needs of the population they serve.

The private sector also has an essential role to play, particularly when it comes to employment and job training. Employers can provide opportunities for returning citizens by adopting "Ban the Box" policies, which remove questions about criminal history from initial job applications, thereby reducing the stigma attached to formerly incarcerated individuals. In Florida, the "Ban the Box" initiative has gained traction, with several private companies and municipalities adopting policies to encourage fair hiring practices. Large corporations and small businesses alike can also partner with workforce development programs to offer job training and apprenticeships tailored to individuals leaving prison, helping to close the employment gap and foster economic stability.

Furthermore, the private sector's engagement extends beyond employment. Businesses can invest in community-based initiatives and public-private partnerships that provide housing, healthcare, and education for returning citizens. For example, in cities like Miami, there are public-private housing initiatives aimed at providing affordable housing options for individuals coming out of prison, offering them a stable environment to rebuild their lives.

The key to successful collaboration is building trust among these different stakeholders. Each sector has its own priorities and challenges, and fostering partnerships requires open communication and a shared vision for addressing the systemic issues associated with reentry. Government agencies can set the stage by creating policies that incentivize private sector involvement and funding for community organizations. In turn, community organizations can leverage their grassroots connections and advocacy power to hold government entities accountable for implementing fair and effective reentry programs. The private sector, by engaging in socially responsible business practices, can help reduce the barriers to employment and housing that returning citizens face.

In Florida, fostering collaboration between these sectors has been critical in advancing reentry initiatives. However, there remains work to be done to ensure that this collaboration is consistent across all regions of the state. Creating formal networks where government, community organizations, and businesses can regularly communicate and strategize will be essential in scaling successful programs. By combining resources, knowledge, and effort, these stakeholders can bridge divides and build the trust needed to create lasting change in the lives of returning citizens.

Investing in reentry programs and support services is a crucial component of reducing recidivism and helping formerly incarcerated individuals transition back into society. Without adequate support, many people leaving prison face enormous challenges, from finding stable housing and employment to addressing mental health and substance use disorders. In Florida, where reentry has become a key focus in recent years, targeted investments in reentry programs can make the difference between a successful return to society and a cycle of re-incarceration.

One of the most effective ways to reduce the likelihood of recidivism is through comprehensive reentry programs that address multiple aspects of a returning individual's needs. These programs, when adequately funded, provide returning citizens with access to job training, education, mental health care, substance abuse treatment, and housing assistance. In Florida, reentry initiatives such as the Transition from Prison to Community Initiative (TPCI) aim to create a seamless transition from prison life to community reintegration by connecting individuals to vital resources before they leave prison. However, such programs require substantial investments from both public and private sources to ensure they are effective and accessible to all individuals leaving the correctional system.

One of the main challenges in investing in reentry services is the need for sustained, long-term funding. While there are state and federal grants available for reentry programs, these are often temporary and contingent on political priorities. Sustainable funding models need to be developed to ensure that reentry programs can continue to operate even when political winds shift. This is why some of the most successful programs combine public funding with private investment, leveraging corporate partnerships, non-profit involvement, and philanthropic contributions to create a diversified funding base. This kind of collaborative funding approach ensures that reentry programs are not only well-resourced but also resilient to changes in government policy.

In addition to securing funding, reentry programs need to provide holistic services that go beyond the immediate needs of employment and housing. Addressing mental health and substance use disorders is critical, as these issues are often underlying factors in criminal behavior. Florida's Reentry Center, which operates out of various locations across the state, provides a model for how comprehensive services can be offered. These centers not only help returning citizens secure employment but also provide therapy, addiction treatment, and support for family reunification. This type of holistic approach is essential in addressing the full range of challenges faced by formerly incarcerated individuals.

Moreover, support services for reentry must be extended to the families of incarcerated individuals. Families often bear the emotional and financial burdens of incarceration, and their role in the reentry process can be pivotal. Investments in family support services can help strengthen family bonds and improve the outcomes for returning citizens. Programs that provide parenting classes, relationship counseling, and financial support can ease the transition for both the individual returning from prison and their family members, making reintegration smoother and more successful.

Investment in these programs is not only a moral and social imperative but also a smart economic strategy. Studies have shown that effective reentry programs reduce the likelihood of reoffending, which in turn reduces the costs associated with incarceration. According to the Florida Department of Corrections, the state spends over $20,000 annually to incarcerate a single individual. By contrast, reentry programs that prevent recidivism can save taxpayers millions of dollars each year. This cost-saving potential makes investing in reentry programs not only an issue of justice but also one of fiscal responsibility.

There are ongoing discussions about increasing state investment in reentry services, particularly in the areas of mental health and housing. Advocacy groups and policymakers alike are pushing for more resources to be directed toward these programs, recognizing that successful reentry benefits not just the individuals involved but society as a whole. To truly bridge divides and build trust, investments in reentry programs must be prioritized at all levels of government and supported by both the private sector and community organizations. This will create a system where returning citizens are given the tools they need to rebuild their lives and contribute positively to their communities.

Creating opportunities for employment and housing is a critical step in ensuring the successful reentry of formerly incarcerated individuals into society. Stable employment and secure housing are two of the most significant factors in reducing recidivism, as they provide a foundation for returning citizens to rebuild their lives and contribute positively to their communities. In Florida, the challenge of securing employment and housing for individuals with a criminal record remains substantial, but there are ongoing efforts and programs designed to address these barriers.

Employment is often one of the greatest hurdles for formerly incarcerated individuals, as many face discrimination from potential employers due to their criminal records. In Florida, over 90% of employers conduct background checks during the hiring process, making it difficult for returning citizens to find stable jobs. However, various initiatives and policies are being developed to help address this challenge. One of the most notable efforts is the "Ban the Box" campaign, which encourages employers to remove the checkbox asking about criminal history from job applications. This gives formerly incarcerated individuals a fair chance to present their qualifications before being judged solely on their criminal background. Several cities and counties in Florida, including Miami-Dade County, have adopted "Ban the Box" policies for public sector jobs, helping to reduce the stigma associated with having a criminal record and expanding employment opportunities.

Additionally, reentry programs often include job training and placement services specifically tailored to the needs of formerly incarcerated individuals. Organizations like Operation New Hope, which operates in Jacksonville, Florida, provide comprehensive reentry services, including job skills training, resume-building workshops, and connections to local employers who are willing to hire individuals with criminal records. These programs not only help returning citizens develop the skills necessary for employment but also build partnerships with businesses that understand the value of giving second chances. In 2019, Operation New Hope reported that more than 1,500 individuals had been placed in jobs through their Ready4Work program, highlighting the effectiveness of such targeted initiatives.

Housing is another significant obstacle for returning citizens. Many formerly incarcerated individuals find themselves homeless upon release, either because they lack family support or because of the legal and financial barriers to securing housing. In Florida, there are various restrictions that limit housing options for individuals with criminal records, particularly in the realm of public housing. Many landlords are hesitant to rent to individuals with a criminal past, and public housing authorities often have strict policies that bar formerly incarcerated people from obtaining housing assistance.

To combat these challenges, some reentry programs in Florida focus on providing transitional housing for individuals leaving prison. These housing programs serve as a bridge between incarceration and permanent housing, offering a stable environment where returning citizens can get back on their feet while they search for employment and more permanent living arrangements. Organizations like The Florida Rights Restoration Coalition (FRRC) provide assistance with housing, helping individuals navigate the often complex and restrictive housing market. By offering transitional housing, these programs reduce the likelihood of homelessness and provide a foundation for individuals to focus on other aspects of reintegration, such as employment and family reunification.

In addition to transitional housing, Florida has also seen growth in permanent supportive housing models for formerly incarcerated individuals. These models combine affordable housing with access to supportive services, such as case management, mental health care, and substance abuse treatment. The Miami-Dade Homeless Trust, for instance, has developed programs that provide permanent supportive housing to individuals returning from incarceration, recognizing that stable housing is a critical component of reducing recidivism and fostering long-term success.

Moreover, public-private partnerships play a significant role in expanding housing opportunities for returning citizens. Some private developers and landlords are working alongside non-profits and government agencies to create housing solutions for this population. For example, Habitat for Humanity in several Florida locations has developed initiatives specifically for individuals who have been incarcerated, offering homeownership opportunities as part of the broader effort to help returning citizens reintegrate.

While much progress has been made, creating more opportunities for employment and housing remains essential for the success of reentry programs in Florida. Both stable jobs and secure housing are foundational to successful reentry, and without them, the risk of recidivism remains high. Investing in these areas and continuing to develop innovative approaches to overcome the barriers that formerly incarcerated individuals face is crucial for building safer, more inclusive communities. By expanding access to employment and housing, Florida can ensure that returning citizens have the support they need to lead productive and meaningful lives, breaking the cycle of incarceration and contributing to the state's overall economic and social well-being.

Public-private partnerships (PPPs) for reentry are a critical approach to helping formerly incarcerated individuals reintegrate into society by combining the strengths and resources of government agencies, non-profit organizations, and private enterprises. These partnerships allow for a coordinated effort that provides a broad range of services, from job training to housing support, mental health care, and mentoring. By leveraging the expertise and financial capacity of the private sector, public-private partnerships can address the significant challenges that returning citizens face, creating more comprehensive and sustainable reentry programs.

In Florida, these partnerships have shown promise in reducing recidivism rates and supporting successful reintegration. One of the most successful examples of PPPs in reentry is the Ready4Work program, which operates in cities like Jacksonville and Tampa. Ready4Work is a collaboration between government entities, such as the Florida Department of Corrections, and private companies, including local businesses and large corporations, that offer jobs, mentoring, and training to formerly incarcerated individuals. Through Ready4Work, returning citizens are provided with life skills training, job readiness programs, and one-on-one mentoring to prepare them for reentry into the workforce. In return, businesses that participate in these partnerships benefit from a well-trained and motivated workforce while also contributing to the community's public safety and economic stability. This collaboration helps address workforce shortages while also giving returning citizens a fair shot at gainful employment.

The private sector's involvement in reentry programs often includes both financial support and direct services. Large corporations such as Bank of America and JPMorgan Chase have funded various reentry initiatives while also providing employment opportunities. Bank of America, for instance, has contributed millions of dollars to support initiatives that focus on second chances, workforce development, and affordable housing for formerly incarcerated individuals. These corporate contributions enable non-profit organizations to expand their services and reach more individuals in need, while the direct hiring of returning citizens demonstrates the companies' commitment to reducing stigma and supporting inclusive hiring practices.

Another example of a successful public-private partnership is the Prison Entrepreneurship Program (PEP), which, although it started in Texas, has inspired similar programs in Florida. PEP collaborates with private businesses to provide entrepreneurship training to incarcerated individuals, preparing them to start their own businesses upon release. The program offers intensive business courses, mentorship from business executives, and post-release support that includes access to financing and networking opportunities. By engaging the private sector in this way, PEP equips returning citizens with the tools and confidence needed to succeed as entrepreneurs, further enhancing their chances of avoiding recidivism and building productive futures.

In addition to employment, PPPs are also vital in expanding housing options for returning citizens. Public housing authorities, non-profit organizations, and private landlords often work together to create transitional and permanent housing solutions for individuals reentering society. Programs like the Miami-Dade Homeless Trust's Housing First initiative, which partners with private developers and landlords, have been instrumental in providing housing for formerly incarcerated individuals who would otherwise struggle to find stable living situations. These partnerships reduce the risk of homelessness, which is a key factor in recidivism, and give returning citizens the stability they need to focus on employment and family reunification.

Additionally, public-private partnerships are increasingly playing a role in providing mental health and substance abuse treatment to returning citizens. Many formerly incarcerated individuals suffer from untreated mental health issues and addiction, which are significant barriers to successful reentry. In Florida, non-profit organizations like The Transition House, which operates in partnership with the state government and private mental health providers, offer comprehensive reentry programs that include mental health counseling, substance abuse treatment, and case management. These partnerships enable the delivery of specialized care that government agencies alone often cannot provide due to budgetary constraints or lack of expertise. By pooling resources, these partnerships ensure that returning citizens have access to the support they need to address the root causes of their incarceration and improve their chances of successful reintegration.

Public-private partnerships also extend to technology and data-sharing initiatives that enhance the effectiveness of reentry programs. For example, technology companies and research organizations often collaborate with government agencies to develop data-driven reentry solutions. These partnerships enable the tracking of reentry outcomes, such as employment rates, housing stability, and recidivism, and help refine and improve the services provided to returning citizens. The Florida Department of Corrections, for instance, has partnered with private technology firms to improve data collection and analysis related to reentry, enabling more effective allocation of resources and tailoring programs to meet the specific needs of returning citizens.

Moreover, public-private partnerships provide opportunities for advocacy and policy reform. Non-profit organizations working in the reentry space often collaborate with private companies to advocate for legislative changes that remove barriers to reentry, such as the expungement of criminal records or the elimination of housing and employment discrimination based on criminal history. These advocacy efforts can have a significant impact on the long-term success of reentry programs as they address systemic issues that prevent formerly incarcerated individuals from fully reintegrating into society.

Developing sustainable funding models for reentry programs is essential to ensure the long-term success and stability of these initiatives. Reentry programs, which provide support to individuals returning to society after incarceration, require consistent funding to offer services such as job training, housing assistance, mental health care, substance abuse treatment, and mentoring. However, relying solely on government funding or short-term grants can be precarious, as these sources may be subject to changes in political priorities or economic conditions. Thus, creating diversified and sustainable funding models is critical to maintaining the effectiveness of reentry services over time.

One of the primary approaches to achieving sustainability is through diversified funding streams, combining government support with private-sector investment and philanthropic contributions. In Florida, for example, reentry programs often receive funding from federal and state governments through agencies such as the Florida Department of Corrections and the U.S. Department of Justice. However, to reduce the risk of budget cuts or shifting political priorities, reentry organizations increasingly seek private-sector partnerships and foundation grants to supplement government funds. Corporate social responsibility initiatives, in which companies invest in social causes, have become an important source of funding for reentry programs. For instance, JPMorgan Chase and Bank of America have been involved in funding workforce development and reentry initiatives aimed at providing employment opportunities for returning citizens. This corporate engagement not only helps fund programs but also fosters job placement partnerships that benefit both businesses and individuals seeking reintegration.

In addition to private sector support, foundations, and non-profit organizations play a vital role in sustaining reentry programs. Foundations such as the Ford Foundation and Open Society Foundations have provided significant grants to reentry initiatives across the U.S. and in Florida, particularly for programs that focus on criminal justice reform and workforce development. These grants often allow reentry programs to expand their services, scale their operations, and pilot innovative approaches to reintegration. Moreover, by supporting data-driven evaluations, foundations help ensure that reentry programs can measure their impact and make improvements, further increasing their chances of securing continued funding.

Another strategy for sustainable funding involves developing social impact bonds (SIBs), which are innovative financial instruments that attract private investment in public programs. SIBs allow private investors to fund social initiatives, such as reentry programs, with the promise of receiving returns based on the success of the program in achieving specific outcomes, such as reducing recidivism rates or increasing employment among returning citizens. If the program meets its predetermined goals, the government repays the investors with interest, creating a performance-based funding model. In Florida, there have been discussions around exploring the use of social impact bonds in criminal justice reform, and while the concept is still relatively new, it holds potential for scaling successful reentry models without over-reliance on fluctuating government budgets. This model encourages accountability and ensures that programs are both effective and efficient.

Public-private partnerships (PPPs), as discussed earlier, also play a crucial role in sustainable funding. These partnerships often combine public funds with private sector resources to deliver reentry services. The private sector can offer financial investment, in-kind contributions, and expertise, while the government provides institutional support and regulatory frameworks. This collaboration helps reduce the financial burden on any one entity and creates shared responsibility for successful outcomes. An example is the Ready4Work program in Florida, which benefits from funding by the state government as well as contributions from local businesses and non-profits. The diversified funding model ensures that the program can continue to provide comprehensive services to returning citizens, including job placement and mentoring, even in the face of budget constraints.

Non-traditional funding models, such as fee-for-service arrangements, can also enhance the sustainability of reentry programs. In this model, reentry organizations charge fees for specific services provided to the government or other institutions, such as training programs, counseling, or housing services. These fees, often reimbursed through contracts with state or local governments, help cover operational costs while incentivizing performance. Fee-for-service models are becoming more common as state governments seek ways to outsource essential services to specialized non-profits, allowing reentry organizations to maintain financial independence while delivering high-quality support to formerly incarcerated individuals.

Another vital element in developing sustainable funding models is fostering community engagement and grassroots support. Fundraising campaigns, donations from local businesses, and volunteer contributions can provide supplementary funding and reduce operational costs for reentry programs. Community buy-in also helps raise awareness of the challenges faced by returning citizens, encouraging local stakeholders to invest time, resources, and advocacy efforts in supporting reintegration initiatives. Crowdfunding and community-driven campaigns have become particularly useful tools for raising funds for specific reentry projects, such as transitional housing or job training programs, allowing programs to expand without being overly reliant on external grants.

Finally, establishing endowments and reserve funds can provide long-term financial stability for reentry programs. By creating a pool of invested capital, endowments generate a steady income stream through interest and dividends, allowing programs to fund ongoing operations even during periods of financial uncertainty. Many non-profits and educational institutions rely on endowments for sustainability, and this model could be applied to large-scale reentry programs to ensure that services continue uninterrupted, regardless of external economic conditions.

In conclusion, sustainable funding models for reentry programs must prioritize diversification, innovation, and community engagement. By combining government support with private sector investment, philanthropic grants, performance-based funding mechanisms like social impact bonds, and grassroots fundraising, reentry programs can maintain the financial stability necessary to provide consistent and effective services to returning citizens. These models not only ensure the longevity of reentry initiatives but also enhance their impact on reducing recidivism, promoting successful reintegration, and improving public safety.

Chapter 23
The Continuation of Voice

The journey of incarcerated fathers is one that doesn't end with their release. Their struggles, triumphs, and stories continue to shape not only their lives but also the lives of their families and communities. This chapter aims to emphasize the ongoing challenges faced by these men and the critical need for continued advocacy and support to ensure that their voices are heard long after their release. The transformation of these fathers from individuals marginalized by society to agents of change and responsibility is a story worth sharing and, more importantly, one worth sustaining.

For incarcerated fathers, the struggles often begin well before they enter prison and persist long after their release. From disrupted family connections to the stigmatization and systemic barriers faced upon reentry, their challenges are multifaceted. In many cases, incarceration strains their relationships with their children, creating emotional distance and trust issues. Fathers who are separated from their children often struggle to maintain an active presence in their lives, leading to feelings of guilt, shame, and a sense of failure as parents.

One of the primary struggles incarcerated fathers face is the loss of parental rights and the challenge of rebuilding their relationships with their children after release. Many incarcerated fathers are noncustodial parents, meaning that their children are often placed in foster care or remain with the other parent during their imprisonment. According to the National Resource Center on Children and Families of the Incarcerated, more than 1.7 million children in the U.S. have a parent in prison. For these fathers, reestablishing their role in their children's lives requires overcoming legal and social hurdles. Many find it difficult to regain custody or even visitation rights, making reintegration into the family unit an uphill battle.

The lack of access to parenting resources and programs in prison compounds these issues. While some prisons offer parenting classes or family counseling, these services are not universally available, leaving many incarcerated fathers ill-equipped to handle the emotional and practical challenges of parenting upon release. Furthermore, the emotional toll of incarceration—combined with the societal stigma attached to formerly incarcerated individuals—makes it difficult for these men to reintegrate into their families and communities effectively.

Despite these struggles, many incarcerated fathers demonstrate remarkable resilience. Programs like the "InsideOut Dads" initiative, which operates in prisons across the U.S., including in Florida, have shown the potential for incarcerated fathers to grow and learn from their experiences. These programs aim to strengthen father-child relationships by providing inmates with the skills and emotional tools necessary to reconnect with their children. Fathers who participate in such programs often report a renewed sense of purpose and a commitment to being more present and involved in their children's lives. The success of these initiatives highlights the importance of continued support, even after a father's release, to ensure lasting change.

One significant triumph for incarcerated fathers is the gradual recognition of the importance of family connections during incarceration. Research has shown that inmates who maintain close relationships with their families are less likely to re-offend. This recognition has led to reforms in some prison systems, such as allowing more frequent and meaningful contact between incarcerated parents and their children. In Florida, for example, the Department of Corrections has implemented video visitation programs to facilitate family connections, especially for those inmates who are housed far from their families. This type of reform acknowledges the critical role that family plays in the rehabilitation process and helps mitigate some of the emotional distance created by incarceration.

The ongoing journey of incarcerated fathers is filled with both setbacks and victories. While systemic challenges persist, the courage of these fathers to persevere in the face of adversity is a testament to their determination to change. Their stories of resilience provide hope that, with the right support, they can overcome the challenges of incarceration and rebuild their lives and families.

The Need for Continued Advocacy and Support

As the struggles of incarcerated fathers persist both during and after their time behind bars, the need for continued advocacy and support cannot be overstated. Advocacy efforts play a critical role in raising awareness about the specific challenges faced by incarcerated fathers, driving policy changes, and ensuring that these men have the resources and support necessary for successful reintegration into their families and communities.

One of the core reasons continued advocacy is essential is the systemic nature of the barriers that incarcerated fathers face. These men are often marginalized by policies that fail to consider their unique circumstances. For example, child support systems frequently overlook the realities of incarceration, leading to mounting debt that fathers cannot realistically pay while in prison. Upon release, many find themselves financially crippled by this debt, making it difficult to find stability, secure housing, or provide for their children. Advocates have long pushed for reforms to these systems to better reflect the economic challenges faced by incarcerated fathers and to prevent a cycle of debt and recidivism.

In addition to financial challenges, incarcerated fathers often face legal and social obstacles when attempting to reestablish relationships with their children. Many fathers lose parental rights while they are incarcerated, and the process of regaining custody or visitation can be long and complicated. Continued advocacy is crucial to ensure that policies are in place to facilitate family reunification when it is in the best interest of the child. This includes pushing for reforms that prioritize family-based services during incarceration and offering legal support for fathers seeking to reconnect with their children.

Nonprofits and community organizations have stepped up to fill some of these gaps, providing incarcerated fathers with essential services like parenting programs, job training, and emotional support. However, these efforts are often underfunded and lack the resources necessary to reach all those in need. Advocacy efforts must focus not only on policy reform but also on securing sustained funding for these critical programs. For example, programs like "Fathers Behind Bars," which provide parenting education and family reunification support, have shown promising results in reducing recidivism rates and strengthening family bonds. Ensuring that these programs receive long-term funding is key to breaking the cycle of incarceration and creating lasting change.

Furthermore, continued support is necessary at every stage of the process—from incarceration to reentry. At the same time, some prison systems have begun to offer more family-focused programs, and many incarcerated fathers are still released into communities without the tools or support they need to succeed. Reentry programs that specifically address the needs of fathers can provide them with crucial support in areas like employment, housing, and legal assistance. Programs such as those run by the Osborne Association and the Center for Urban Families have been instrumental in providing formerly incarcerated fathers with these services, helping them rebuild their lives and maintain connections with their children. However, expanding access to these programs remains a significant challenge, particularly in underfunded and underserved communities.

On a broader scale, advocacy for incarcerated fathers must also involve raising awareness among the general public. Too often, the experiences of incarcerated fathers are overlooked or misunderstood, contributing to the stigma that surrounds them upon reentry. Advocacy organizations must continue to push for public education campaigns that highlight the importance of supporting these fathers in their journey to rehabilitation and reintegration. By changing the narrative around incarcerated fathers and focusing on their potential for growth and positive change, advocates can help foster greater understanding and compassion from the public.

Policy advocacy also remains crucial in addressing the root causes of mass incarceration and the specific challenges faced by incarcerated fathers. Legislative changes, such as the 2018 First Step Act, which aimed to reduce recidivism and improve conditions within federal prisons, are steps in the right direction. However, more work is needed at both the state and federal levels to ensure that policies reflect the needs of incarcerated fathers and their families. Advocates must continue to push for reforms in sentencing, parole, and family law to ensure that these men are given a fair chance to rebuild their lives after release.

A Final Call to Action

As we come to the end of this journey through the struggles, triumphs, and enduring hopes of incarcerated fathers, one thing is abundantly clear: change is not only possible; it is necessary. These fathers are not just statistics or names in a system; they are human beings—men who have often made mistakes but who also possess the capacity for growth, redemption, and love. Their stories are a call for compassion, justice, and a collective responsibility to ensure that no one is forgotten, no matter how dark their past may seem.

The experiences shared throughout this book highlight the deep injustices and systemic flaws within the criminal justice system. Incarcerated fathers often face insurmountable barriers, not only during their imprisonment but also upon their release, as they struggle to reconnect with their families, rebuild their lives, and contribute to society. These men are caught in a cycle that perpetuates poverty, trauma, and isolation—yet, with the right support, they can break free from these chains. We have seen, time and again, that when fathers are given the tools to heal, grow, and reconnect with their children, the ripple effects are profound. Families heal. Communities heal. Society becomes stronger.

This is a call to every reader, every community member, every advocate, and every policymaker: the time for action is now. We can no longer turn a blind eye to the struggles of incarcerated fathers and their families. We must use our voices to advocate for change—whether it's pushing for policy reforms, funding crucial reentry programs, or simply extending a hand of empathy to someone who has been released from prison. The transformation starts with us, with individuals who are willing to step up and say, "These men deserve a second chance. These families deserve to be whole again."

We must hold our lawmakers accountable, demanding that they prioritize criminal justice reform that addresses the root causes of incarceration and supports the rehabilitation of incarcerated fathers. This includes the implementation of trauma-informed care, equitable sentencing, and the expansion of reentry services that focus on family reunification, job training, and mental health support. Advocacy organizations cannot do this work alone—they need allies, they need communities, and they need you.

For community members, this is a call to open your hearts and minds to the realities faced by formerly incarcerated individuals. The stigma they carry is often a heavier burden than the punishment itself. By offering understanding, compassion, and tangible support—whether that's mentoring, providing job opportunities, or helping with housing—each of us can play a role in their reintegration. A small act of kindness or acceptance can change the trajectory of a father's life and, in turn, transform the future of his children.

For faith communities, this is an invitation to live out the principles of forgiveness, redemption, and love that many of us hold dear. Incarcerated fathers need spiritual guidance, mentorship, and a safe space to process their pain and seek forgiveness. Faith-based organizations have a unique role to play in fostering reconciliation within families and helping men find the moral and spiritual compass they need to lead better lives.

And finally, for the incarcerated fathers themselves: your stories matter. Your struggles, your pain, your efforts to rebuild are all part of a larger narrative of resilience and hope. Don't give up on yourselves. Continue to fight for your families, for your futures, and for the chance to become the fathers you've always wanted to be. Know that there are people out here—people who believe in your potential, who are advocating for you, and who want to see you succeed. Your journey is not over, and with each step you take toward healing and rebuilding, you are making the world a better place for your children and for generations to come.

This final call to action is a plea for unity, for compassion, and for the courage to change a broken system. The voices of incarcerated fathers must not fade into the background. Their stories must continue to inspire us, to motivate us, and to push us toward a future where justice is not just about punishment, but about restoration and healing. Together, we can break the cycle. Together, we can create a world where every father has the opportunity to succeed, every family has the chance to heal, and every child can grow up with the love and support they deserve. The time to act is now. Let's not wait any longer.

Bonus
Story 1

This may not be your story, but it is a story experienced by hundreds of thousands of fathers incarcerated like myself— fathers whose will and resolution stand firm, whose hearts are fixed on putting to rest a past lifestyle for the sake of a child far more worthy than any worldly affections.

After countless mistakes and repeated stints in solitary confinement due to multiple assaults, extortion, and excessive gang activity, Yahweh delivered me. He revealed that not only am I worth more than a meaningless lifestyle, but so are my family and child.

To the fathers and mothers behind barbed-wire fences and steel doors who can relate—I strongly encourage you to be courageous enough to let your child be the motivation for your transformation. Just as the author himself once told me, I now pass his same message forward to you: allow your child to outweigh an unpromising life. Leave the ninety-nine sheep behind and go after the one that needs you most.

To my daughter, Alyvia—I love you deeply and miss you so much. I dedicate this passage to you. Your beating heart is the driving force behind my transformation, from being a rebellious man and gang leader to becoming Yahweh's follower. I have exchanged my pain for purpose, my disconnection for connection, and my resentment for forgiveness and freedom—all on the path to finding you. I will continue to let you be my guiding light through dark times as I press forward and navigate my way back home to you.

To my brothers and sisters of all denominations who struggle with hopelessness, I pray that my unshackled voice inspires you to find the bravery to leave behind a life of self-destruction for a life of fulfillment.

Finally, I extend my deepest gratitude and admiration to the author, whom I consider a true friend and mentor. His book, Unshackled Voices, spoke volumes—loud enough for deaf ears to hear. I sincerely encourage the world to read it with faith, knowing that it may bring you the same revelation that I have received.

To everyone supporting this message—thank you all. Stay strong in faith, and as always, **PRAISE YAHWEH!**

Daddy loves you, Lyvi.

Vince

Bonus
Story 2

I t's a sad situation when my only consolation is the expectation of another life. These were the words staring back at me from the graffiti-scrawled steel bunk as I lay on my stomach, chin resting on my forearms. I was in the Northwest Florida Reception Center—a pit stop on my way to death row at Florida State Prison. I was two weeks shy of my 21st birthday, and I felt like America had thrown me away.

Just hours earlier, I had been sentenced to death. I had watched my loved ones break down as the sentence was pronounced, and then I saw those words etched into the bunk. They caught my attention in a way nothing else could at that moment. The prosecution's argument for my execution was purely business:

"If we sentence this 'man' to death, I believe we can have him in the electric chair within four years. It wouldn't waste much of the taxpayers' money housing him."

Again, I was only 20 years old. The thought of a second chance, in some other life, was appealing.

My first walk down a death row wing was an experience in itself. The cell doors were just bars—no solid doors to shield you. But the unspoken rule was clear: Don't look into a man's cell when you walk by. Of course, this curious and nervous kid knew nothing of that rule. As I peered into these rooms filled with infamous serial killers, one thought struck me and never left: I am one of the condemned.

I was now among those deemed unfit for society, those labeled beyond redemption. I took that to mean I was uncivilized—less than human. And in the eyes of the system, the only answer was to put me down like an animal.

But today, I thank Yahweh for being the true author of my story—for not leaving me in the hands of men.

Today, I am a 48-year-old father and grandfather. I am a man of faith. I have been forgiven, just as I have forgiven. And now, my life has purpose. I can't rewind time or undo my past, but today, I plant and water the seeds of change.

This experience has shaped me into a tool that can be used by society. I have a passion for helping at-risk and proven-risk youth. But more than passion—I have experience and solutions. I've endured the fire of Florida's prison system and emerged refined. I've participated in every program and class that could contribute to my growth. I've even created programs of my own, and the results are undeniable.

But what is the end result?

Is it just so I can be a better inmate?

Will I ever have the opportunity to pay it forward in society?

Can I make a difference in the life of the next Samuel Williams? Right now, he stands at the crossroads, just as I once did. I wish I had a me when I was standing there.

Florida commuted my death sentence—or at least prolonged it. My sentence now states that I must die in prison. I suppose that means I am still being thrown away.

America still eats its babies without taking the time to taste what they are consuming.

Our lawmakers are put in place by the people. They are the voice of the people.

So, who are the people?

Yes, I meant to put them in there.

Samuel Ben Israel

Bonus
Story 3

A t 19 years old, my voice was silenced when I was sentenced to three natural life sentences. The weight of those words caught in my throat—how could I logically serve such a term? I had spent more years in prison than I had in society, written off prematurely because of my immaturity. I had always believed that America's laws were based on biblical principles—an eye for an eye. Yet, I had not taken a life, and still, I was systematically sentenced to a slow death behind bars. Life without parole may not be death by lethal injection, but in many ways, it is an even harsher sentence.

In the criminal justice system, death sentences are scrutinized at multiple levels through the appeals process, but life sentences are often handed down without the same oversight. State attorneys push for maximum penalties, and judges have little discretion in sentencing. I was represented by a public defender at trial, but once found guilty, I couldn't afford appellate counsel. I was left to navigate this system alone.

Ignorance and immaturity shaped my mindset, influencing my actions. At 40, I finally found my voice—one I had lost in my adolescent years. I had been unable to hear the voice of Yahweh, drowned out by the noise of uncertainty, fear, and poverty. My father was taken from me in a racially motivated act when I was just a year old. I grew up in a home filled with anger over his absence, surrounded by broken environments that skewed my perception of the world. I saw my fellow delinquents as family because, in my mind, I belonged nowhere else. Without a father figure in the home, I never understood what it meant to truly have one.

Even after receiving my sentence, my outlook remained unchanged—until I heard the voices of my own children. My son would ask, "Dad, are you really coming home?" My daughter, longing for my presence, once told me with heartbreaking finality, "If you're not at my graduation, just forget it—I'm giving up on you."

For years, I had promised my return. Now, she was in high school, and those promises felt empty.

Then, I heard the words of my grandfather echo in my mind:

"The life of a man is seen in one of three stages—construction, destruction, or reconstruction."

Those words played in my head for weeks. I knew I had to change.

After two decades behind bars, my vision is clearer than ever. My time is now dedicated to breaking old mindsets and rebuilding myself. My thinking has changed, my actions have changed, and I am committed to applying the knowledge I've gained. I don't want to just give my children advice—I want to be present in their lives. A father's words have power, but his presence is even more meaningful.

When I first entered prison, I was denied access to many educational programs because of my lengthy sentence. The administration believed that, since I would never return to society, I had no need for an education or a trade. Even after earning college credits from Valdosta Community College, I was banned from continuing my studies. Yet, I pursued every self-improvement program I could, not for rewards or better living conditions—there were none—but for my own self-correction.

If I were truly irredeemable, if I were truly a menace to society, would I have chosen integrity and personal growth?

Although there have been policy advancements, there is still much work to be done. I have changed, but the system must change too. Why spend millions of taxpayer dollars on rehabilitative programs if they will never be applied outside of prison walls? Justice should not be one-size-fits-all.

We live in a nation that once condoned child labor and chattel slavery—atrocities that we now view as unacceptable. The same must be said for the inhumane practice of excessive sentencing. It is time for new amendments. The same way we reexamine our past, we must challenge the present. The blindfold must be removed from Lady Justice so that she may see the reality of the system she governs.

America was built on ideals of liberty and equality, yet we have forgotten the voices of the founding fathers. Perhaps it is time we have a conversation with them today.

Nechemyah Ben Israel

Author's Note

We would like to give thanks to God Yahweh for Allowing us the Vision to be leaders in this Movement. We Are advocates for our fellow incarcerated Brothers who are seeking a righteous path to redemption. We ask each family, all civilian supporters, and all prison volunteers to please keep our movement in prayer. We know all that one Day Soon our voices will be heard. The power Of Yahweh Will turn the hearts of the fathers to the children and the children back to the fathers. This book looks to Generate a vision of transformation.

It is to highlight the fact that fathers are overcoming Obstacles, to better themselves, and praying for opportunities to pay it forward. As productive members in the society which we once health helped destroy. Through grace, we have witnessed the awesome power of Yahweh, and have become living testimonies that restoration and Retribution Can be our story as much as it can be yours.

To all my fellow Incarcerated brother's ~

No matter what your faith is:

Israelite, Christian,

Muslim, Jewish, etc.

Stay on your righteous journey Allowing the Most High To be your beacon of light, Helping you to navigate through the waters of life in the darkness of nights. Continue to chart your course as a God-fearing man seeking to be found Worthy of a second chance of freedom. Remain faithful in your charitable service to the unshackled Voices of incarcerated father's movement. Please continue submitting the transformational Testimonies of your life.

Our goals as God -Fearing men Is to encourage change in all men who currently embrace Immoral ways, so those ways don't influence our children to embrace the same dark roads We once traveled. Our voices break courses as messages of Yahweh.

For those who wish to learn more or get involved, please reach out to our team at:

Unshackled Voices <unshacklevoices@gmail.com>

Unshackled voices of Incarcerated fathers:

P.O. Box 51565

Ft. Myers, Florida

Thank you to everyone who supports our cause. Your love and dedication are truly appreciated.

With love and respect,

Yarah Ben Israel & Samuel Ben Israel

www.ingramcontent.com/pod-product-compliance
Lightning Source LLC
Chambersburg PA
CBHW062101080426
42734CB00012B/2717